PULL THE STICK OUT OF YOUR @$$

PULL THE STICK OUT OF YOUR @$$

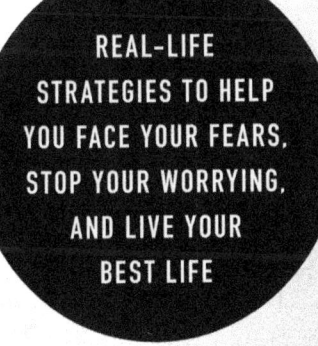

REAL-LIFE STRATEGIES TO HELP YOU FACE YOUR FEARS, STOP YOUR WORRYING, AND LIVE YOUR BEST LIFE

BRUCE SERBIN

IMPORTANT DISCLAIMERS!

Mental health is a serious topic. This book is based on my personal story and recovery and should not be used in place of expert medical care. Do not self-diagnose yourself. Always consult a medical professional or mental health professional before making changes to your medication, therapeutic routine, or any part of your recovery.

This book contains adult language and content that is not suitable for children.

This book is dedicated to my friend Richard Zoly. You were taken from this world way too soon and I miss you every day. I know you're throwing the biggest and wildest parties up there in heaven. Thank you for teaching me how to pull the stick out of my ass, how to have fun, and truly enjoy life. It was the best thing I learned in college.

© Copyright 2020 – Bruce Serbin

All rights reserved. This book is protected by the copyright laws of the United States of America. No part of this publication may be reproduced, stored in or introduced into a retrieval system, or transmitted, in any form or by any means (electronic, mechanical, photocopying, recording or otherwise), without the prior written permission of the publisher. For permissions requests, contact the publisher, addressed "Attention: Permissions Coordinator," at the address below.

Published and Distributed by
SOUND WISDOM
PO Box 310
Shippensburg, PA 17257-0310
717-530-2122

info@soundwisdom.com

www.soundwisdom.com

While efforts have been made to verify information contained in this publication, neither the author nor the publisher assumes any responsibility for errors, inaccuracies, or omissions. While this publication is chock-full of useful, practical information, it is not intended to be legal or accounting advice. All readers are advised to seek competent lawyers and accountants to follow laws and regulations that may apply to specific situations. The reader of this publication assumes responsibility for the use of the information. The author and publisher assume no responsibility or liability whatsoever on the behalf of the reader of this publication.

The scanning, uploading and distribution of this publication via the Internet or via any other means without the permission of the publisher is illegal and punishable by law. Please purchase only authorized editions and do not participate in or encourage piracy of copyrightable materials.

Cover design by Eileen Rockwell

ISBN 13 TP: 978-1-64095-165-5

ISBN 13 eBook: 978-1-64095-166-2

For Worldwide Distribution, Printed in the U.S.A.

1 2 3 4 5 6 / 22 21 20

CONTENTS

You Look Like You Have a Stick in Your Ass!................. 13

Part 1: Stick-Pulling Strategies 19

How Do You Begin to Remove the Stick?.................. 20

Chill the F*ck Out!... 28

Clean Out Your Ears and Listen!............................35

Don't Be a Know-It-All...39

Know When to Ask for Help................................ 44

Don't Be Full of Shit... 48

Shut Your Mouth and Stop Complaining!..................52

Mean People Suck—Don't Be One of Them................57

Mind Your Effing Business 62

Be More Accommodating..................................... 66

Stop Planning Everything.................................... 69

Do Something You're Not Supposed to Do 74

Fantasize about the Craziest Stuff You Can Dream Up.... 80

Don't Waste Your Time with New Year's Resolutions...... 84

Don't Let the Quest for More Kill You 89

Don't Put Others Before Yourself 98

Don't Rush to the Grave..103

Don't Shit on Yourself 107

To Hell with Conformity— Be Who You Really Are 114

Laugh at Yourself—It's the Key to
    Disarming Others 121

Follow Your Heart and Everything Else Just Follows......124

Don't Quit Your Day Job.......................................128

Envy Can Be Your Best Friend if You Use It Right 132

Get Over Your FOMO Because the Party
    Is Always Where You Are.................................137

When Life Throws You Lemons, Just Say "Screw It"....... 141

Stop Asking Why.. 144

Hell Yeah!—Profanities Help..................................147

Some Tips to Flip... 151

When You Don't Know What to Do, Just Get Started 154

Part 2: Protecting Your Mental Health 157

Emotional Pain Is the Biggest and
    Most Dangerous Stick in the Ass.......................158

Mental Illness Is Not a Death Sentence 164

Holy Hypochondriac 169

Spread Your Wings and Fly 174

I Have Something to Say but I'm Social Phobic 182

Taking Medication Doesn't Mean You're Weak...........189

Find Safety and Comfort in Yourself.......................193

This Is How You Tell Anxiety to F*ck Off 199

Part 3: Reflections on Life and Parenting and Some Other Random Thoughts from Bruce **207**

Birthdays Rock! 208

Ho Ho Ho, Oh No, Not the Holiday Season 211

You're Never Really Ready to Be a Parent 215

Some Other Random but Important Stuff 221

Don't Sit on It:
  Pull That Stick out of Your Ass Immediately! 227

Mental Health Resources **231**

National Suicide Prevention Lifeline 232

Crisis Text Line 232

Anxiety and Depression Association of America 233

National Alliance on Mental Illness 233

The National Institute of Mental Health
  Information Resource Center 234

The Anxiety and Phobia Program at
  St. Vincent's Behavioral Health Center 235

Acknowledgments 237

Introduction

YOU LOOK LIKE YOU HAVE A STICK IN YOUR ASS!

> The root of being uptight is our unwillingness to accept life as being different, in any way, from our expectations.
> —Richard Carlson

I was 13 years old the summer I attended sleepaway camp in Massachusetts. I was at an age when boys started looking at girls a little differently. They weren't gross. They didn't have cooties. They were changing. We were changing. All of a sudden, we wanted to be with them. Being "cool" meant having a boyfriend or girlfriend. It was new. It was different. It felt right.

One of many memories of anxiety getting in my way

We had camp dances on some nights, a time when boys and girls would come together, hang out, dance, and just have fun. One night, this girl tapped me on the shoulder and asked me to dance. "Me?" I asked, kind of surprised. I wasn't exactly the dancing type. I didn't know how to dance, and I figured everyone would just laugh at me. Unfortunately, she was serious. My friends kind of egged me on to do it, so I reluctantly made my way onto the dance floor.

After what was probably not even a minute but felt like a lifetime, this girl didn't seem too impressed. I don't blame her. I was nervous. I couldn't dance. I was shaking. I was pretty sure all eyes were on me, even though they weren't. I wasn't any fun. I knew it wasn't going well, and finally she said, "You need to loosen up. You look like you have a stick in your ass!" Then she walked away. Def Leppard's "Pour Some Sugar on Me" would never sound the same again.

Unfortunately, this is one of many painful memories I have of when my anxious personality got in the way, ruined something good, and left me depressed. I suppose this particular instance was even more memorable because of how blunt she was, saying I had a stick in my ass. As hurt and upset as I was, she was right: I did have a stick in my ass.

What does it mean to have a stick up your ass?

Well, perhaps you might be picturing someone walking around with a great big stick hanging out from his bottom. But in modern times, it's simply an expression for someone who is a tightwad—someone like that young boy on the dance floor who was a complete trainwreck.

For years, both before and after that camp dance, I had a huge stick jammed up my ass. I was the poster boy for anxiety, the one who made the biggest deal about everything. It got in the way of everything I did. I was always so quiet, nervous, and preoccupied with the thoughts in my head. I worried about what other people thought of me, constantly playing out different scenarios in my mind, trying to script out every interaction with people ahead of time, a perfectionist, a bit obsessive and compulsive, a hypochondriac. I didn't think I was worthy of great things and never expected them, and so much more. Worst of all, constantly having that big stick up my ass made me sick and, I believe, is one of the reasons that I suffered with extreme anxiety and panic attacks for so many years.

I've spent 20 years studying mental illness and speaking with experts on it.

Because of my own battle with mental illness, I've spent the last 20 years studying it closely, specifically anxiety disorders and depression. The way the mind works and how that influences our behavior and actions has captivated me beyond my wildest imagination. Not only that, but as a publicist I've had the opportunity to work with and represent a number of the nation's top psychiatrists, psychologists, and other mental health experts. Speaking with them daily about mental illness and prepping them for media interviews has been an unbelievable learning experience.

I've lived with mental illness, been sidelined by it, studied it, and worked with the best experts on it. It's my goal to share all that I've learned over the years and put it into a fun and informative book that's easy to read.

Although I like to think I made a complete 360 and am no longer uptight, I'll be the first to admit that even now there are days I still find a stick in my ass, albeit usually a much smaller one. That's okay though, because occasionally it serves me well, making me cautious and careful when I need to be. It becomes a problem when you don't know how to remove the stick from your ass and you're living with a big one lodged up there all the time, like I was.

Aren't you being disrespectful telling people they have a stick in their ass?

If you haven't noticed by now, this is a very different kind of book that takes a lighthearted approach to some serious topics. Let me be perfectly clear about something: I am in no way trying to downplay the severity of mental illness by trying to be funny and saying I had a stick in my ass. Mental health is a matter of life and death for many people and needs to be treated promptly and by a professional. It is perhaps one of the most important topics in our society today. When I talk about having a stick in my ass, I'm simply using that as an analogy to describe the behavioral side of my anxiety disorder, or the parts that I could learn to change and control. I am not referring to the brain chemistry, chemical imbalance, or hereditary component that are outside of one's control.[1]

My main goals in writing this book were fivefold:

1. To point out the fact that we all need to lighten up, which I refer to in my book as "pulling the stick out of your ass."
2. To raise awareness that despite all our differences, we are really all the same.
3. To remove the stigma around mental illness.
4. To push love and equality for all mankind regardless of gender, religion, sexual orientation, skin color, or anything else.
5. To help anyone who is struggling and can benefit from my own mental health battles, mistakes, challenges, and successes.

I wish you the best in your life journey and hope for the utmost happiness and success to come your way.

My very best,
Bruce Serbin

---

[1] I'm not a doctor, and this book is not intended to provide medical advice. As with any advice book, you should speak with the health professionals in your own life—who know you best—before making any important changes.

Part 1
STICK-PULLING STRATEGIES

HOW DO YOU BEGIN TO REMOVE THE STICK?

> The best cure for a stick up your butt is a dog to play fetch with.
>
> —Ryan Lilly

How many sticks are stuck up your ass at this moment in time? Do you:

- Get really upset when something goes wrong, however small it may be?
- Complain regularly?
- Bullshit people with a fake persona or words unsupported by actions?
- Find it difficult to relax in social or professional settings?
- Fill your mind with negative self-talk?
- Overanalyze every situation thinking about what you could have done differently?

How Do You Begin to Remove the Stick?

- Obsess about what other people are doing or achieving?
- Stick your nose in other people's business and then gossip about it?
- Feel the need to plan everything down to the most minute detail?
- Find it difficult to make changes in life because of worry, fear, and/or self-doubt?
- Cope with stress by being overly critical of those around you?
- Dominate conversations and/or talk down to people?
- Make resolutions or set goals just for the hell of it but then never follow through?

If you answered yes to one or more of these questions, then you, my friend, have at least one stick up your ass. Uncomfortable, isn't it—that feeling of pressure caused by being too uptight, anxious, and critical of yourself and/or others? Your life could be dramatically improved by removing the sticks from your derrière and learning to live in a more present, less judgmental, and less uptight manner.

Part one of this book provides strategies for removing the obstacles currently blocking you from a fulfilling, authentic life. But first, let's address what you're not going to get in this section: traditional motivational garbage about your mindset completely dictating your reality, and that's because...

Positive thinking and motivation are often bullshit.

I was feeling down a while back because my company's billing was a bit lower than it had been at the same time in the previous year. I told a motivational speaker friend of mine about it on the phone, and he said, "Just change your thinking, Bruce. Expect more clients. Expect more money. Expectations become reality." I wanted to reach into that phone and put my hands around his neck.

I clearly understand what my friend was getting at. He meant well and was trying to help. Unfortunately, his advice was meaningless. Positive thinking on its own is not the answer. Positive expectations on their own are not the answer. These things hide the pain while distracting us from the real issues at hand. What about the effort? What about doing more things to get more work and increase my billing? Magical thinking isn't going to make it somehow happen. While I'm at it, I'll just magically expect one million dollars to all of a sudden flood my bank account, because I'm sure that will happen, too. If thinking happy thoughts were the answer, then everyone's problems would just disappear. I've also been thinking a lot about world peace, but apparently my positive thoughts aren't having much of an impact on that either.

There are more books, articles, and keynote speeches on the topic of positive thinking than you can imagine. A quick glance at the shelf in the bookstore or a brief search online will reveal more information on the topic than you ever wanted to know. But the majority of it is wrong or misleading.

I struggled—and still struggle—with negative thinking at times. I've read more self-help books on the topic and represented so many self-help and personal development authors in the media who write about positive thinking. Many of these people are well-intentioned. However, even the ones who mean well can be so misguided.

Positive thinking is a great concept. After all, negativity sucks. I'm all for thinking the best and being optimistic. The problem is, the self-help gurus all want you to believe that positive thinking is as easy as snapping your fingers. They tell you things like, "Change your thinking to change your life," and "You can attract greatness and become rich and successful just by changing your thinking." Bullshit. What a bunch of malarkey! Pull the stick out of your ass and get real. It's not that simple. (Am I thinking negatively?)

Again, positive thinking is a wonderful concept, but there's more to it than manifesting your happy thoughts.

Let's say you're struggling with negative thoughts. Maybe you're beating yourself up. Maybe you're doubting your confidence when it comes to your work or some area in your personal life. Guess what? Telling yourself how amazing you are, that you're the greatest in the world, that you can do anything you set your mind to (*in a really upbeat motivational speaker voice*), and on and on and on, isn't going to change a thing. Think about it: all you're doing is lying to yourself, and your brain can see it as clear as day. It's talking back to you, saying, "Cut the crap!"

Realistic thinking is the answer.

While having a positive attitude is great, deluding yourself by trying to change a negative thought into the world's pleasantest and most comfortable-sounding sentence is a fairy tale. It's unrealistic, and therefore it's not going to make you feel better.

The answer is realistic thinking. It's taking your negative thoughts and changing them into ones that are closer to reality, which will help you see the honest truth.

For years I struggled with flying. Nobody would ever think that about me because now I love flying and I'm obsessed with airplanes. But yes, there was a day when getting on an airplane was nearly impossible, and when I did make it on, it was often a very uncomfortable situation.

Naturally, I had a lot of negative thoughts when it came to flying. Most people told me to try positive thinking. I would try so hard to change my mindset, and it frustrated the crap out of me that it didn't work. It made me feel worse because I thought I had a bigger problem.

Not only am I suffering from negative thinking, but now I'm the one guy who isn't going to be helped by positive thinking! After much frustration, I realized that there was nothing wrong with me. I needed to stop lying to myself. Instead of telling myself how great this flight was going to be and that I'll feel fine, I started using realistic thinking.

Example

> **Negative:** "Oh shit, I have to fly tomorrow. I can't do it. What if I freak out, have a panic attack, and make a fool of myself?"
>
> **Positive:** "You can do it! You're going to feel great. Nothing can stop you."
>
> **Realistic:** "Yup, I have to fly again. It might not always be the most comfortable thing in the world, but each time I learn something and it gets a little easier. I'll try to stay busy by watching TV, playing a game, or talking to the person sitting next to me. I'm going to do the best I can."

The next time you find yourself struggling with negative thoughts, remember: don't try to sugarcoat things by turning your situation into something it's clearly not and may never be. Don't listen to the motivational speaker bouncing around the stage like the Energizer bunny telling you that all you have to do is become a positive thinker. Be honest and realistic with yourself.

The truth is, negative thoughts always consider the worst-case scenario in everything. Luckily, the worst case rarely ever happens. It could—and acknowledging that possibility is realistic thinking—but it usually doesn't. The other thing to realize is that realistic thinking on its own isn't going to solve the world's problems. It can help you feel better and see things more clearly, but changing your thinking isn't always the quick answer. It's simply a piece of the larger puzzle.

Supplement realistic thinking with action to support actual change.

As I've reiterated throughout this chapter, changing your thought patterns will help remove any sticks from out of your rear end, but it's not the only strategy you need to implement to become a less anxious, uptight person. The rest of the chapters in this section detail various principles for loosening up and living a more laid-back life. As you'll discover, most of them are action oriented, meaning that you have to do the work to change your behaviors along with your perspective of your environment. Some may help you more than others; read them all, test them out, and figure out what combination of stick-removing strategies works best for you. And if your neuroses derive from more than simply being wound too tightly—if they are symptomatic of an anxiety disorder—then part two of this book will provide insight and support in getting help for mental illness.

CHILL THE F*CK OUT!

> The most wasted of all days is one without laughter.
> —e. e. cummings

Someone asked me the other day how it is that I'm so laid back about most things. I kind of laughed. It made me think of how things used to be. I was quite the opposite, actually. Worry was ingrained in me, and I couldn't just snap my fingers and turn it off like some people can. I had a major worry stick up my ass, and this is one I'm proud to say I pulled almost all the way out. In fact, I might have gone too far because sometimes people say I look like I don't give a shit about anything.

Part of the challenge was that I was born into it. My wife and I joke sometimes that despite how great my family is, worry tends to be a central theme of many conversations. When you are raised in this environment, you just assume that's how it's supposed to be. In fact, I would say it just became so embedded into my subconscious that there was no time to make a choice to worry about something or not. I just did.

A little worry is helpful; a lot of worry is dangerous to your health.

The good news is no matter how bad it is, regardless of how worried you are and how shitty it makes you feel, you can learn to pull the worry stick out of your ass and live with minimal worry. I say *minimal worry* because to say *no worry* would be unrealistic and, in fact, worrying a little is good for you. It keeps you alert and on your toes.

The worrying I'm talking about is constantly obsessing about events in the future that typically are outside of your control. For example: Let's say I had to take a flight. Although I love flying now, at one point many years ago I was a terrible flyer. Weeks, maybe even months before that flight, I was thinking about it non-stop: *What if the plane crashes? What if there's a lot of turbulence? What if I freak out?* The flight could be a month away, and I was unnecessarily making myself sick.

When I was a kid, my mom was diligent about our annual physicals. I worked myself up so much weeks before the appointment. I didn't like going to the doctor and getting poked. I also feared they were going to tell me I had some horrible incurable disease. When the big day came, they couldn't take my blood pressure until the checkup was over and I knew everything was okay.

Now, like I said, things are very different. Little by little, I started changing for the better. I learned to pull the worry stick out of my ass, reduce the amount of concern I experienced, and just let life play out. I learned how to chill the f*ck out. It's hard to pinpoint an exact reason for this shift; I think it was probably a culmination of several things:

- **Going off to college and being around new people** who were much more laid back than I was. I met a lot of fun party animals who were always having a good time and didn't worry about much, and while probably not the best influence on my schoolwork, in the long run it was one of the greatest things to ever happen to me because it changed me for the better.
- **Repeatedly landing in the ER because of a huge panic attack.** This kept happening over and over again. One doctor told me I had to learn to lighten up and work through the stress because it wasn't good for my health. Those words have always stuck with me.
- **Becoming an adult.** I realize the older I get, the more shit happens. I can either let it get the best of me or laugh it off.
- **Inadvertently learning mindfulness strategies**. When you're truly connected to the present

moment, aware of your surroundings and what's taking place right now, that's what mental health professionals refer to as mindfulness. I didn't make it a point to practice mindfulness specifically, but I think that's what I learned to do.

All these factors—and probably a few others—enabled me to stop taking everything so freaking seriously. The truth is, there's a time and a place to be concerned about things, but the majority of our worrying is a complete waste of time, a drain on our energy, and a danger to our health.

Shit happens…roll with the punches.

It was my daughter's 13th birthday. We were having a big party for her at her favorite Mexican restaurant. We had 30 of her friends coming and some other people. My wife got this big balloon that had the numbers 1 and 3 (put together it was 13). We were getting out of the car at the restaurant, and all of a sudden, we hear, *POP!* The 3 was gone. There was silence, and we all just looked at each other.

Now, we could have had a major freak-out. I knew my wife was going to be upset, and I was hoping my daughter wouldn't be. I knew my seven-year-old son was just going to laugh. So, after a few awkward seconds that felt like hours, I finally said, "Well, I guess you're turning one today." Thankfully, everyone laughed.

Shit happens, and it usually happens when you least expect it. Granted, losing half a balloon wasn't really a big deal and certainly wasn't a life-or-death situation, but it could have put a damper on the rest of the evening if we had let it. Luckily, we didn't.

The truth is, most things aren't as big of a deal as we make them out to be. Things go wrong—and sometimes they can go very wrong—but the important thing is how we respond to the problems.

When things go wrong, you have two choices:

1. Lose your cool.
2. Pull the stick out of your ass and go with the flow. This is by far the best thing you can do. Don't get mad. Don't freak out. Take a couple deep breaths. Say a few choice words to yourself. Just make do and carry on.

Will it always be easy? No. Will it always be as minor as a balloon popping? Of course not. One day it could be spilled coffee all over your work papers, a canceled flight, a lost iPhone, or something really serious. All kinds of things will go wrong in life; that's unavoidable. However, you can control your reaction to it, and that's what makes all the difference.

I don't know where you are in your life when it comes to how seriously you take things and how much you get worked up worrying about the future. If you are anything like I was, you know how much it sucks. Nothing good comes from being a tightwad and not being able to let loose. If that's you right now, changing this is one of the best things that you can do for yourself. You're going to feel better. Things that had such a strong grip on you are going to dissipate. Your stress will diminish. You're going to feel great, and people are going to be more attracted to your new personality. The following strategies will help you take the stick out of your ass and loosen up:

- **Take the "I don't give a shit" pledge.** Like that song in *Frozen* says—just "let it go." Whatever you are worried about, make the decision once and for all just to pull the stick out of your ass and let it go. Your worrying is doing you no good. Practice being more laid back about things and see what a difference it makes. (You're welcome for getting that song stuck in your head.)
- **Step back.** It's easy to get consumed by worry. When you start analyzing every little detail and playing out every possible scenario in your head to the point that you feel sick over it, just stop and walk away. I even have a little stop sign I used to carry around with me to help me remember this.
- **Be prepared.** When you are prepared, the worry tends to subside. Very important: There's a major difference between being prepared and obsessing. When you know what could happen, you're ready for it, and you've made the decision to just

let happen whatever will happen, that's the right way to approach things. But when you dwell on every possible scenario and feel sick over it well in advance, that's the wrong way to do it. Be prepared, but leave it at that.
- **Know that uncertainty exists and is normal.** Nobody knows what the future will bring and some things are completely out of your control. It's pointless to worry about these things that might not even happen.
- **Realize that your anticipation is usually worse than the actual event.** I can't tell you how many times I made such a big deal over something, and when it came time to do whatever it was that I was freaking out about, it wasn't that bad. That's because anticipation is usually much worse than the actual event itself. We create the wildest, craziest, and scariest stories in our mind that quite often are completely unrealistic.
- **Face your worries.** The more you face the things that bother you, the less power they hold over you. It's not easy, but it is necessary. Plus, nothing builds your confidence and self-esteem more than overcoming your fears.
- **Do things to help you relax.** Exercise, slow your breathing, find a quiet place to relax, or do something else that helps you regain your composure. Whatever it is that relaxes you, just do it more.

CLEAN OUT YOUR EARS AND LISTEN!

> One of the sincerest forms of respect is actually listening to what another has to say.
> —Bryant H. McGill

Many years ago, I attended this speed dating event where you spend two minutes chatting with each person in the room and then reconnect with the people with whom you hit it off. I had really great chemistry with this one woman, except I couldn't remember her name. Needless to say, she wasn't impressed, and I felt like a complete idiot.

Even nowadays, my wife often thinks I have trouble listening and remembering important details. I admit that on some days, I don't hear a lot of what she tells me, especially when it involves chores or errands. Generally speaking, however, I think I do an okay job listening, and it's definitely something I have gotten good at since I don't do the bulk of the talking in most conversations.

Being quiet can be an asset.

As I've already said, people say I'm quiet. That might have something to do with my introverted personality or that at times I can be quite a social phobic. While these aren't necessarily characteristics for which I am thankful, they have served me well because they make me a better listener.

The world is full of people who love to talk, but the world is not full of people who listen well. When you sit back and stay quiet while someone else is rambling on, you actually learn a lot from listening to their words and watching their mannerisms and body language. In fact, it's often how I can judge rather quickly whether or not I like someone and I'm going to jive with them, or if they are going to be a royal pain in the ass to deal with.

Did you ever encounter someone who is a big talker? They tell you everything about their childhood, their favorite food, favorite restaurant, favorite movie, solve all your problems that you don't even have, and so much more in the first 10 minutes of meeting them. I prefer to go the other way. I'm a big fan of the 80/20 Rule of Communication, which is 80 percent listening and 20 percent speaking, and it fits my personality to a T. It also works really well in a business setting and even casual interactions. It helps you quickly assess people and situations, get a feel for what's really going on, find solutions, and more.

Listening well helps you be more present and relaxed.

While it is possible to contribute to a conversation and listen well at the same time, you can't totally dominate a conversation and listen well. Becoming a better listener will help you in all that you do. Next time someone gives you crap about being quiet, tell them to relax because you're just being a good listener. Below are some strategies for improving your listening skills.

- **It's all in the name.** One of the biggest things I am working on when it comes to meeting people is remembering their name. After all, it's the least you can do—and yet also the most important. I used to be terrible at this, as evidenced by the speed-dating story above, and sometimes I still forget someone's name. It's really embarrassing when it happens, especially when it's someone prominent or a person you want to get in good with. Make it a point to remember their name.
- **Repeat what they just said.** If you have trouble remembering details or need to remember something especially important, repeat it back. For example, if you tend to forget names, say their name when you give yours. "Hi Jane, I'm Bruce." Repeat what they just said: "Really, you find that a lot of people do..., because I have noticed...."

- **Write it down.** When the person you are speaking with says something important, write it down or make a note in your phone. Granted, you can't always just whip out a pen and paper or your mobile device, but when you can, it can be a great tool to help you remember important details.
- **Ask questions.** This is a great strategy that can help you not appear so quiet and socially awkward. It can also make you a much better listener, help you remember details, and will impress the people with whom you are speaking. Even generic questions work well: *How did you get started in this? Why do you think most people enjoy it? What mistakes do most people make in this area? What changes do you see coming to this in the future?* Don't forget the basic *who, what, where, when, why,* and *how* questions.
- **Clear your mind of clutter.** It's hard to listen to anyone when you're preoccupied and have a million things going on at once. If you can't reschedule an important meeting for a time when you're feeling better and thinking clearer, do the best you can to put down everything else that's going on at that particular moment so you can focus on the person in front of you.

DON'T BE A KNOW-IT-ALL

> A know-it-all is a person who knows everything except for how annoying he is.
> —Demetri Martin

I was at a party with my wife, and there was a small group of us hanging out. I was being my usual quiet self, but that was fine because this one guy wouldn't shut up. He kept running his mouth about everything. He seemed to know all about meteorological conditions and weather patterns, as well as how to take apart a car engine and then put it back together again, and he filled us in on all the celebrities he had met. He seemed to have knowledge, stories, and personal experiences with everything in the world. After a while, I wasn't buying it.

Over the course of your life, you're going to encounter all different types of characters, but one of the most annoying by far—and one of the ones with the biggest stick up his ass—is the know-it-all. You know the type:

constantly runs his mouth, pretends to know everything, and sometimes even talks down to those he considers less informed.

What's even funnier about the know-it-all is that most of the time he doesn't even know what he is talking about! In fact, more times than not, he has no clue. He's a tricky one because he's learned to talk a good game and sound convincing. A closer listen, however, reveals nothing more than opinions and generalizations stated in a very emphatic way.

On the flip side...

Many times, people will hesitate to contribute to a conversation for fear of being seen as the know-it-all. I used to do this all the time. What I learned—and what you need to understand—is that there is a big difference between someone who is really knowledgeable about something and someone who is a know-it-all.

If you are genuinely smart, talented, or have detailed knowledge about a topic, you should never hold back your ideas. Other people need your gifts and can make drastic improvements in their own lives based on your insights and expertise. In fact, everyone typically has that one thing that they just know everything about—or at least way more than the average person. By all means, talk away. The know-it-all, on the other hand, seems to have specialized knowledge about everything under the sun, and he won't let you forget it.

The reason for the know-it-all's behavior comes down to a few things. Usually, it's a personal insecurity of some type. Sometimes it's based on a past experience where the person was embarrassed about not knowing something, and to make sure that never happens again he is always angling to be seen as the smart one. For others, being the know-it-all is about having control or stems from being previously left out. Sometimes it's the result of a few different causes, but it's always a behavior that's rooted in fear.

The following are some strategies to help you productively respond to a know-it-all:

- **Don't let it get to you.** When you encounter a know-it-all don't take it personally. This is not a result of anything you did. It's always something that the know-it-all is going to have to work to overcome.
- **Be ready for a fight.** If you disagree with the know-it-all, be ready, because he usually won't let you get away with not thinking that his way is the best way.
- **Choose your words wisely.** When disagreeing with the know-it-all you can help yourself by carefully selecting the words you say. Start off with something like "Great idea, and I think we

can do even better by…" Or, "I like that, but I was also thinking we could…"

- **Sometimes it's best to do nothing.** If it's a situation where I'm never going to encounter this person ever again, I usually just keep my mouth shut, get to the end of the interaction, and leave as quickly as possible. In this case, there's no reason to make the situation any more difficult, because even if you try to disagree, it probably wouldn't do much good.
- **Sometimes it's best to joke about it.** Let's say the know-it-all is one of your friends, and you want to say something without pissing them off. You can nonchalantly say something like, "Dude, shut the hell up." Or, "Girl, you like to run your mouth." They'll start to get the point.
- **Tell them the truth.** If the know-it-all is someone who is going to be in your life on a regular basis and you are at the point where you just can't take it anymore, it's time to say something. Be nice but to the point—something like: "You know, I like you, but you are acting like a know-it-all." When you reach this point, if you really want the know-it-all to change his behavior you just have to say it like it is. Hopefully he gets the message. If not, it's not your problem and you just have to move on. Think of it this way: until someone stands up to the know-it-all, he's never

going to change his ways. You can hopefully be that person who brings about change.

You're not fooling anyone.

If, on the other hand, you happen to be the know-it-all, it's time to pull the stick out of your ass. You're not fooling anyone. In fact, just about everyone can see right through you. If you're doing it for attention and because you want to be liked, it's actually producing the opposite effect and turning people off. People are attracted to confidence, but being a know-it-all crosses the line into cockiness—and nobody likes that.

If you're the know-it-all or you feel pressure to be a jack of all trades, pull the stick out of your ass, drop the act, and closely examine the root cause of this problematic behavior.

KNOW WHEN TO ASK FOR HELP

> We can't help everyone, but everyone can help someone.
> —Ronald Reagan

Back in the day, my parents would spend a lot of time in teacher conferences, and year after year, they would hear the same thing about me: "Bruce doesn't ask for help when he's struggling." I used to be one of those people who wanted to do everything by myself even if I didn't know what the hell I was doing. Paint the house? Yeah, I got this. Make a lasagna from scratch? Of course I can. Put a new roof on the building? Yep, I'll find a way. I would rather have suffered and made a bad situation worse than ask someone who knew more than I did for help.

There is absolutely no reason for trying to take on the world by yourself.

I'm not sure what changed—probably marriage and living with someone who wouldn't put up with it—but

Know When to Ask for Help

one day I pulled the stick out of my ass and didn't feel like singlehandedly taking on the world. After all, we are living in the collaboration economy, so I guess I wanted to collaborate.

Don't get me wrong: I still get enormous satisfaction from completing a project by myself, even if that means it won't come out as well or will take me 10 times longer than if I had worked with others. However, I'm not a young fool anymore, and I know when to ask for help. In fact, you could even accuse me of asking for too much help sometimes. For example, I'm technologically challenged. I don't understand the first thing about computers, other than how to type on them. I constantly ask the tech-savvy people in my life for help. I don't know how to back up and update my iPhone so I ask my wife to do it for me.

Yes, perhaps with certain things I should get off my ass and make an attempt. I'm not going to deny that. But other times that's not the case and asking for help is the way to go.

My point is, life is hard enough on its own. If you don't know what the hell you're doing, stop being so damn stubborn and just ask for help. I get it: you're cocky and want to prove to the world that you are Mr. or Mrs. Independent and there's nothing you can't do. Get off your high horse, pull the stick out of your ass, and stop suffering. Would you rather your project come out like garbage, which causes more work not only for you but for other people, or would you rather it get done right?

Pull the control stick out of your ass.

- Start by researching and trying to find information about the things with which you're less familiar. Maybe you can figure it out on your own.
- When it becomes pretty obvious that you don't stand a chance at the task staring you in the face, get help. There's no reason to suffer through something when you don't know what you're doing just for the sake of being able to say you did it all by yourself or to try to impress others.
- If someone shows you how to do something, then you can go off and do it all by yourself the next time.
- Some people love to lend a helping hand, while others won't give you the time of day. If you have a run-in with the type of person who has a stick up their ass and doesn't want to be bothered, screw them. Find someone else who is willing to help.

By the way, if you're ever at a job interview and the recruiter asks, "What is one weakness you have?" this is a great topic to talk about. Say something like, "I love to take on projects by myself. I guess you could say my weakness used to be that I wasn't good at asking my colleagues for their input. Although I still get the satisfaction of completing tasks on my own, I know that in order to get the best results it takes a team effort." They will freaking love you! It shows them that you are a self-starter but that you also know how to be a team player. Trust me, it works.

DON'T BE FULL OF SHIT

> One of the few times in a man's life when he is not full of shit: the morning of a colonoscopy. Enough said!
> —Jim Lawrence

Did you ever come across someone and think: *My God, this person is really full of shit*? Bullshit is rampant these days, even in those who aren't know-it-alls. You don't have to look very far to find it. In fact, it's sad to say, but when you meet someone who is truly genuine and not full of shit, it makes you wonder: *Did I miss something? Where's all the bullshit?*

We've all been full of shit at one point (or many) in our lives.

The reality is we've all been full of shit at one time or another. If you've ever used an online dating service, you've surely experienced the surprise that is meeting a match for the first time who looks nothing like their profile picture. Perhaps you're even that person using a profile picture that's from ten years ago, when you were a little thinner, a little less wrinkled, and had more hair. We all embellish a little bit—in an attempt to fool other people, sure, but also to bullshit ourselves into thinking we're not aging.

Even people you love and care about are full of shit to some degree. Your mom, the wonderful lady who loved you, nurtured you, and brought you into this world has been full of shit before. Maybe you didn't get accepted to the college of your choice. Maybe a girl broke your heart. Your mom was always there for you, saying, "It's all going to be okay." No, Mom, you're full of shit! You're just trying to make me feel better.

Your best friend, the one you confided in because he swore he would never tell anyone was full of shit when he went and blabbed your deepest thoughts and secrets to your other friends. Your teachers, coaches, boss, employees, and other people in your life are full of shit many times, too.

Guess what? Even you—yes, you—have been full of shit somewhere along the way, if not today. Did you make New Year's resolutions to lose weight and get healthy once and for all? Bullshit. Is this the year you're going to start saving money? Nope, you're full of shit.

Eliminating the bullshit altogether would be impossible and would probably make you a big jerk. Below are some ways to at least start to pull the bullshit stick out of your ass somewhat:

- **Don't overpromise.** You know those people who promise you the moon and the stars? They're full of shit. Promise only what you can truly deliver on. Actually, I prefer to under-promise and then over-deliver. This way there's no trace of bullshit and you seem more credible.
- **Don't cover a lie with another lie.** This is what we teach in crisis communications 101. People love to cover a lie with another lie, and the bullshit train continues. Rather than perpetuate the bullshit once you're busted, you should come clean, apologize, and say what you're going to do to fix the problem and never let it happen again.
- **Compliment but offer alternatives.** White lies are just another form of bullshit, but sometimes they're your only option. If your spouse asks you, "Does this dress make me look fat?" well, I'd be bullshitting you if I said there was a right answer, because there's not. If you say, "No," they're going to accuse you of just trying to make them feel good. If you tell them, "Yes, it makes you look fat," they're going to dismember you and kick you to the curb. I always try to lead with a compliment and then offer other alternatives. "Wow, you look smoking hot. You also have that blue dress that really accentuates your eyes." Similarly, let's say you just sat through a terrible

45-minute presentation at work. Afterward, your boss asks you, "What did you think?" Obviously, the no-bullshit response would be, "It sucked!" Of course, you might also be out of a job. Instead, try saying, "It was pretty solid, but something you can do to make it even better is..."

Bullshit is all over the place. Try to pull the bullshit stick out of your ass by eliminating it as much as you can. Sometimes you just can't, and that's how it goes, but try to do your part to help reduce the amount of bullshit in the world whenever possible.

SHUT YOUR MOUTH AND STOP COMPLAINING!

> Complaining not only ruins everybody else's day, it ruins the complainer's day, too. The more we complain, the more unhappy we get.
>
> —Dennis Prager

When you're standing in a long line, there's always that one guy who won't shut his mouth and is going on and on complaining about everything. The line is moving too slow. He's hot. The staff doesn't know what the hell they are doing. Or maybe you're in a restaurant and the food and the service are clearly exceptional, but there's that lady sitting at the next table who has a problem with everything. She is bitching to the waitress that the food is cold, the service is slow, and people are talking too loudly even though that's not the case at all. You know the type of people I'm talking about. I hope you're not one of them. When they start in, you just want to say, "Pull the stick out of your ass and shut up!"

Don't be a jackass.

Let's be perfectly clear: there's a difference between standing up for what's right and acting grumpy and pissed off because you have nothing better to do than be an asshole and boss people around. I'm all for getting good service and having things done right, especially when I'm paying. But acting bossy and snobbish, pushing others around, being mean-spirited, barking orders, and just giving people a hard time is ridiculous and uncalled for. The worst offenders are those who complain when there is absolutely nothing to complain about. You know the people. They simply want to let their voices be heard. They're mean, hurtful, out to give you a piece of their mind (even though you didn't ask for it), and they try to ruin your day.

I watched an encounter like that recently, and it was mind-blowing to see how bad-mannered and obnoxious some people can be. I was on a flight and this lady in the row in front of me was a total nightmare. She had the window seat, and a passenger sat down beside her and said hello. She said, "Please don't talk to me. I'm very busy." Before the flight attendants served drinks, they made an announcement that on these short flights where they operate regional jets, they offer only coffee or water. The passenger shook her head in disappointment and went on to order a Bloody Mary. The flight attendant, very politely, said, "I'm sorry, ma'am. We don't stock tomato juice or any alcohol on these short regional flights." The lady went off on the flight attendant. I felt so bad for the flight attendant. After the flight, I asked her if she was alright and apologized for the passenger's rude behavior. I told the flight attendant she should have unleashed her fury on the lady and said, "Ma'am, were you not listening to the effing announcement prior to our beverage service? Open your ears."

There's a time and a place for the right complaint.

People sometimes say that I let others get away with too much or that I don't speak up and complain enough. That's actually not true. When someone needs to be spoken to or I have a right to complain, you better believe I will. The difference is I try to look at the bigger picture, put myself in the other person's shoes, and attempt to determine where the problem is really originating from. Most of the time, acting like a jerk to the first person I encounter isn't going to fix the problem. Not only that, but when you act like an asshole and treat others like crap, then they really are going to be less inclined to help you.

I know there are some topics I might complain about in this book, but that's my right because after all, it's my book! But for the most part, complaining is a major stick in your ass…and in everyone else's, too. Here are some tips and tricks for pulling this stick out of your ass:

- **Complain only when you really have to.** Complaining for the sake of complaining is just going to make others not like you because you're such a negative person and not fun to be around.
- **Complain only when you think that something realistically can change.** Most of the time when we complain, we're complaining about things we can't control or that aren't going to change no matter how much complaining we do. If you're stuck on the tarmac during a weather delay, for example, complaining is absolutely pointless because you can't control Mother Nature. Neither can the flight attendant, pilot, air traffic controller, or anyone else.
- **Know when to keep your complaint to yourself.** Even when something is really frustrating, most of the time complaining will only make things worse. In the weather delay example above, none of the authorities on board could affect the time of takeoff, so complaining would not do you any good. In fact, it would only ruffle feathers, because nobody else wants to hear it.
- **If you are going to complain, make sure you're talking to the right person or department.** I realize that sometimes you have to work your way up the chain of command, but save

yourself some time and aggravation by attempting to get to the right person as soon as possible. There's nothing worse than taking 10 minutes to go through your entire story only to hear, "I'm actually not the person who can help you with this. Let me transfer you to..."
- **Realize that complaining is bad for your health.** Complaining releases the stress hormone cortisol, which raises your blood pressure and blood sugar and has a host of additional side effects. This can increase your risk of heart disease, diabetes, obesity, and other conditions.
- **Learn how and when to complain effectively.** There's a time and a place to make a comment that yields results versus acting like a complete asshole and belittling people.

As the late Aretha Franklin said, it's about R-E-S-P-E-C-T. Show a little, and you'll be amazed how far it will get you.

MEAN PEOPLE SUCK—DON'T BE ONE OF THEM

> Being mean about other people isn't on my radar.
> —Geri Halliwell

I can't stand mean people. Mean people have a really big stick shoved up their ass.

The other day I was in the supermarket. Yes, I like doing the food shopping in our family. It relaxes me. I was heading for the checkout lane at the same time that this other lady, who was coming from the other direction, was also looking for an open line to pay for her groceries. Our eyes locked and I knew what was about to happen. I was obviously much closer to the checkout line than she was, so she purposely sped up to get there before I did. I could have (and maybe should have) said something to her, but I let it go. When she was finished and it was my turn, the cashier told me she saw the whole thing and was shocked I didn't go off on the lady because she clearly cut in front of me.

Here's the thing: the world is full of mean people. Mean people suck. I'm not sure why exactly people are mean. Maybe it's their personality. Maybe they were born that way. Maybe it's a sign of an underlying issue. I don't know. All I know is that being mean isn't acceptable behavior, period.

Now yes, I have my moments too, where maybe I'm in a bad mood and snap at someone, or maybe I'm on a deadline and rush someone through a conversation. I'm not perfect. Nobody is. Overall, I think—and I've been told—that I'm a really nice guy. Even when a telemarketer calls, which is terribly obnoxious, I don't sit there and chat with them, but I'm not a jerk either.

We're all in this together.

The point is, we're all in this together. Why make it any more difficult than it has to be? Some things are outside of our control, but how we act toward other human beings is something we can all work on improving. Besides just being nicer in general, the following are some specific kind things that are so simple you can start doing them today:

- Hold the door for people.
- Say "please" and "thank you."
- Listen more.

- Always remember the Golden Rule of treating people how you want to be treated.
- Ask permission before you do something that will affect other people.
- Compliment people more.
- Show interest by asking questions.
- Remember the details.
- Surprise someone.
- Lend a helping hand.
- Do something nice just because.

How to handle an asshole...

If you encounter someone who is mean, break the cycle of negativity with the following principles:

- **Be nice to them.** When someone is mean to you, it's tempting to act like an asshole right back to them. It's actually the knee-jerk reaction of many people. Try not to stoop down to their level. Just because they have a stick in their ass doesn't mean you should act like them. In fact, do the opposite. Not only will responding with kindness make you the bigger person; it will make you feel good about yourself.
- **Don't be a pushover.** Responding with kindness is all well and good, but don't let them take advantage of you. Accepting a mean remark here and there without saying anything is one thing,

but allowing it to happen frequently is another. That's called being a pushover. If someone is repeatedly nasty or insulting, gets physical, calls you names, or does anything else inappropriate, stand up for yourself and fight back. If you let them walk all over you, they are just going to keep acting the same way.
- **Try to be empathetic.** Some people really don't want to be mean, but their behavior is the result of something much larger that's going on or has gone on in their life. Try to be understanding and see where they're coming from. Sometimes they just want a friend and someone to listen to them. Sometimes you can help them. Other times you can't. Of course, if the person is an asshole because that's just who they are, then don't waste your time with them, which leads me into my next point...
- **Don't associate with mean people.** If someone is simply a mean and toxic person, it's not doing you any good being around them. Get away from them and find better people to associate with. There are plenty of fish in the sea. If you're in a setting where that's difficult to do, like school or work, have as little contact as possible with that person.
- **It's not you. It's them.** When you are in the presence of a mean person, they'll try their best to put all the blame on you. No matter what is going

on, it will always be your fault, or they'll want you to believe your actions are to blame. They'll belittle the things you do and take every chance they can to cut you down. Don't buy into this for even a second. It's not you. It really is them.

The unfortunate thing about mean people is that sometimes they convert other nice people into unkind people just by transferring their negativity to those with whom they associate. Have empathy and show kindness toward mean people, but don't let assholes cause or worsen any sticks in your ass. Being nice to others is a surefire way to lessen your anxiety and enjoy your life more.

MIND YOUR EFFING BUSINESS

> If it doesn't involve you, it shouldn't concern you.
> —Unknown

One of my really close friends is in a polyamorous relationship. In other words, he is married and has a girlfriend. In fact, they all live together and care for each other. Another close friend of mine is in an open relationship. He is married, but he and his wife are able to date and sleep with other people. Both of these friends are the nicest people you could ever know. More importantly, they are both extremely happy and have rock-solid marriages. Those kinds of relationships might not be ideal for me, but it's not my place to tell them how they should live their lives. Ultimately, if they're happy, then I'm happy for them.

The gossip mill needs to downsize.

I live in a fairly small city where gossip runs rampant. It's the kind of place where everyone has to know each other's business—and worse, they have to comment on it. It drives me nuts.

A really nice couple with whom I'm friendly recently bought a really big house. I mean, this thing is huge—the kind of place most of us aren't ever going to live in, let alone visit. I was very happy for them. The details of their move weren't any of my business, nor did I really care to know them. The couple was happy, so I was happy for them.

Unfortunately, the gossip mill was in full effect and rumors started flying.

- How could they afford such a house?
- I wonder what kind of money he is making?
- I didn't know he was so successful.
- Who died and left them money?
- Don't they have better things to spend their money on?
- She doesn't work, so where did the money come from?

A similar thing happened when another couple I know decided to get divorced. "Wow, I didn't see that coming," said one lady. "I always thought she could do much better," said another. How did I respond? "Clearly they aren't happy together, and if they chose to get divorced then I support their decision; and ultimately, it's none of my business."

There are a lot of reasons to mind your own business...

- **It has no effect on you.** If someone buys a new car, takes a different job, moves, gets married, does something that you deem stupid, foolish, or anything else, and it has no effect on you, then just stop right there and shut your mouth. Pull the stick out of your ass and stop being so nosy!
- **There's more to the story.** Another reason it's meaningless to speculate about other people's business is because there is much more to the story than you realize—I guarantee it. Just as there are details about you that other people don't know, you don't know every little detail about what other people are doing or going through.
- **It means you're not happy.** If you have to sit there and comment on other people, it's usually a sign of dissatisfaction or conflict in your own life. Before you start talking about others, take a good look in the mirror.
- **What works for one person may not work for someone else.** Being concerned about other people's business is stupid, just simply for the fact that things that work for some people may not work for you. What someone else finds happiness or takes pleasure in, what helps them

overcome a difficult situation or simplifies their life, might seem like a nightmare for you. It's their prerogative.
- **It's downright hurtful.** Speaking poorly about other people is just hurtful, even if it's not directly to their face. Even though it doesn't bother me so much anymore when someone speaks badly about me, it can still be hurtful to most.

Asking questions, speculating, and commenting on other people's business doesn't do you any good. It's a waste of time and energy. Whenever you start to do this, pull the stick out of your ass, come back to your own life, situation, problems, and choices that you make. That's the only thing you should ever be concerned about. What other people are doing, how they are living, what they are spending their money on, or anything else doesn't concern you. Mind your own damn business.

BE MORE ACCOMMODATING

> One person can make a difference, and everyone should try.
>
> —John F. Kennedy

You know what I love about my kids' pediatrician's office? Same-day appointments. They know that kids get sick and need to be seen right away. But amazingly, you can call a dermatologist or any other kind of doctor and you can't get seen for three weeks. "I'm sorry, that big zit on your face will have to wait 21 days for our next available appointment." WTF?

Being accommodating makes life pleasanter for everyone.

The more you can be accommodating of others, the better life is for all of us. After all, it's about helping people out and lending a hand when you're able to. Of course, there are times when you genuinely are so busy that you can't help. And yes, there are times when you don't want to be bothered by your neighbor who needs your help with every problem known to man. I get that.

Generally speaking, however, taking time to accommodate other people is a good thing. The best part about it is that it's reciprocal. When you're in a crisis and need help fast, people are going to remember that time you accommodated them. But if you're an asshole and ignored their need, they're going to remember that too.

My favorite example of being accommodating happens every morning while I'm driving my daughter to school. We always have to drive through this one roundabout. The rule of driving in a roundabout is simple: the car to your left that is already in the roundabout has the right of way. Once there is nobody coming, you can enter the roundabout.

While it's not stated anywhere or written as an actual traffic law, I believe there is an exception to this rule. When you have major traffic coming from all directions and entering the roundabout to the point where people are literally just sitting still in the roundabout, then everyone should be accommodating and let one car in on each side. Some people follow my rule. Others, however, are complete assholes and won't let you in for anything. When they do this, I glare at them for being an asshole. Of course, they already know it.

Maybe the roundabout isn't a matter of life and death and isn't a big deal in the grand scheme of things, but it is a small example of how you can be more accommodating. Sometimes it's just the little things that make the biggest difference.

Oftentimes the small acts of kindness are the most meaningful.

Sometimes I'm at the grocery store and all I need to get is one item. Unfortunately, everyone else in the store has a cart full of food. The right thing to do is to be accommodating. If your cart is overflowing, let me in. I do this all the time when I have a full shopping cart and someone comes up behind me with one item. Again, it's another little example of how to accommodate others.

Does your friend need a ride and you don't need your car that morning? Offer to lend it to her or tell her you'll drive her. Is your spouse not feeling well but has a lot of things to get done? Offer to do what you can to help. Is a neighbor going out of town and has no one to come check on her cat? Offer to do it.

Life is hectic. We're all busy. When you have the chance to be accommodating, help someone else out and make their life a little easier. Don't ask questions; just pull the stick out of your ass and do the right thing.

STOP PLANNING EVERYTHING

> Sometimes we need to stop analyzing the past, stop planning the future, stop figuring out precisely how we feel, stop deciding exactly what we want, and just see what happens.
>
> —Carrie Bradshaw

Many people have tried to swim across the Hoover Dam, but all except one man have died attempting the crazy stunt. Aaron Hughes, a British man attending a bachelor party in Las Vegas, is the first person believed to swim across the reservoir and live to tell the tale.

"I literally just turned to the lads, said 'I'm off,' and they were all cheering me on and I swam across," he told the *Daily Post* in Wales.

I'm not suggesting that you try to swim across the Hoover Dam or attempt any other kind of stunt that could cost you your life. That's just plain stupid. But there is a lesson to be learned from Hughes's accomplishment: sometimes you just have to pull the stick out of your ass, step into the unknown, and take your chances.

Pick up any self-help or personal development book and more than likely you'll find a chapter that discusses the importance of planning. According to popular logic, many big decisions require careful planning and strategizing. Or do they? Think about the last time you had to make a choice or decide on something that was pretty significant. What was the process like? Did you toss and turn about it and lose quality sleep? Did you get knots in your stomach and struggle to eat? Did you have a case of persistent butterflies and jitters? Did you feel like crap constantly?

**Your gut instinct
is often your best guide.**

Now think back to the very first time this choice was given to you. What did your gut instinct tell you to do? In the end, did you end up choosing what you first felt, or did you make a different choice after sitting on it for days on end?

I don't know which way you went with your decision, but I can tell you this: you made yourself sick obsessing over it. It was uncomfortable. It was annoying. It was also unnecessary. Your indecisiveness lodged a big stick up your ass that prevented you from taking action. But then something great happened: your deadline came, whether self-imposed or otherwise, and you were forced to pull the stick out and make a decision. No matter what you chose, just making the decision and putting it behind you took all the pressure off and made you feel a heck of a lot better.

A study published in *Science Magazine* found that people make better decisions if they stop thinking about the pros and cons and let the unconscious mind do some of the work. So, next time you're faced with a big decision, don't sit and deliberate too much. Pull the stick out of your ass and follow your gut.

Overplanning isn't the key to success; it's the key to unnecessary stress.

In addition to making better decisions, here are some other reasons to avoid overplanning:

- **Trying to maintain a set schedule makes it miserable when things don't go according to plan.** A bump in the road will almost always ruin the overplanner's day. Shit happens. Your appointments are going to run late. Your car battery is going to die. You child will get sick. You'll get stuck on a call. Trying to stick to a strict agenda is generally impossible, causes massive amounts of unnecessary stress, and limits your ability to bounce back when plans have to change.

- **It limits creativity.** Telling someone where they need to be, how long they need to be there, and what they need to be doing when they are there hinders innovation. Creativity can't be forced. It just happens. Many very successful ideas have come to life scribbled on the back of a bar napkin or when someone was taking a shower, not when they sat down to think about it.
- **It's not fun.** Sure, I suppose you can plan your fun. But for me, the best fun happens naturally on its own.
- **Too much of a future focus removes you from the present moment.** When you're not in the present, you're missing out on the greatest moments in life.

I was the worst example of an overplanner. I used to have trouble making even the smallest, most insignificant decisions. My mind would become flooded with the "what ifs": *What if I choose this and then this happens? What if I choose that and then this happens?* I was notorious for asking everyone else what I should do, yet I never asked myself. It's a constant back-and-forth battle with no upside, and it leaves you feeling more confused and exhausted.

It's music to my ears when my wife says to me, "You obviously didn't think this through." She says that quite a bit to me. Sometimes her frustration is justified.

Sometimes it's not because I would have made the same decision anyway had I thought about it longer.

If you struggle with focusing too much on planning the future rather than enjoying the present, here are three strategies for recalibrating your perspective:

- Make a commitment to spend less time deliberating or considering your options.
- Recognize that your first instinct is correct more times than not.
- Put less pressure on yourself to make the "correct" decision up front. The reality is that if you make the wrong choice, in most cases things can be reversed or undone.

Plan when you absolutely have to. In general, though, remove the planning stick from your ass because it will drive you crazy and sap you of energy. Nothing good comes from living life in anxiety mode, afraid of the future.

DO SOMETHING YOU'RE NOT SUPPOSED TO DO

> Throw caution to the wind and just do it.
> —Carrie Underwood

Every once in a while, you just have to do something you're not supposed to do. I'm a huge believer in this. I'm not talking about breaking the law or anything illegal. What I mean is breaking away from the way you do things on a daily basis and also giving in to those things that you probably shouldn't be doing but really want to do—indulgences, if you will.

Rules and routines are the treadmill of life.

Everyone needs a break from the set routines into which we've fallen. The mind and body come to rely on certain patterns and behaviors. That's not a bad thing by any means, but you have to be careful you don't fall into stagnation or boredom. You have to keep the fun and excitement coming or else you become disinterested and get lackluster results. This is especially important if you find yourself just going through the motions and feel like you need to find that spark or just break up the monotony. Occasionally breaking the rules is a good idea for many reasons:

- **It builds self-esteem and confidence.** If you are always playing by someone else's rules, you're conforming to someone else's ideals for your life. That's no good.
- **You're thinking outside the box.** If you go through life doing exactly as you are told, you'll be living a very mundane life. Rule breakers tend to be more creative, better problem solvers, and free spirits. They see opportunities where others see chaos.
- **You're acting like a thought leader.** If you follow the rules, you're going about life the same old way everyone has gone about it forever. When you break the rules, you set your own course. You develop your own thoughts, ideas, and philosophies. This is where innovation comes from. You become a thought leader.
- **It's fun.** Let's admit it: being a rule breaker is just downright fun.
- **It's inspiring.** Whenever I've spent time with a rule breaker, it has always forced me to look at

the way I do things in my life and see if there is a better way.

Believe it or not, there are positive and productive ways to break the rules.

My good friend Dr. Alok Trivedi and I were discussing this recently, and we came up with a few examples of how to incorporate some rule-breaking into your life:

- **Eat whatever you want for a day.** Yes, we all know that eating healthy and exercising are important. But once in a while you just have to go wild. For one day, eat whatever you want. If you love Big Macs, head for the Golden Arches. If you want a Chicago-style pizza with all the toppings or an ice cream sundae, then indulge yourself. Comfort food has an important purpose, and giving yourself this sweet reward every now and then will make you feel good. In fact, you'll actually be more likely to stick to your diet the rest of the time.
- **Walk around in your birthday suit.** Do not go out naked in public unless you want to get arrested. But when you are alone in your own home, close the blinds and walk around naked. You're giving yourself permission to let loose, let go of your worries, and be free. To really boost your self-esteem, stand in front of the mirror and

admire what you see. It's healthy to get in touch with your body. Science has even proven that losing the PJs at night helps you get better quality sleep and is healthier for your skin.
- **Act like a child.** As grownups, we're supposed to adhere to a certain level of respectable behavior. But if you ask people when they had the most fun in their lives, over and over again you'll hear it was when they were a child. As adults, we need to connect with our inner child. It sparks our fun side, creativity, and imagination. Just for a day, try not acting your age and see how good it makes you feel.
- **Curse.** Having a potty mouth probably won't impress your boss or your customers, but allowing your words to run loosely when you're alone is good for a variety of reasons. It helps you let off steam and reduces stress. It inspires creativity. It builds self-esteem and confidence because you're going against what's deemed appropriate. It also helps tear down the fear of judgment from others. Studies also show that people who curse tend to be more intelligent. So today, let those F-bombs fly.
- **Buy something nice for yourself.** Saving money is important. But what happens when you turn 100 years old and have a bank account full of money and nothing to show for it? By all means, have a financial cushion—but enjoy life. If you

want to go on that week-long cruise, just go. If you want to spend a little more on the nicer car, do it. We all need money, but if you're not enjoying your money, then you're not living your life. Let go of your fear of money and start enjoying it a little more. Go out and do something nice for yourself today.

- **Be conceited.** Generally speaking, the best advice in almost any situation is to check your ego at the door. But sometimes self-assurance can actually be good for you. Most people tend to downplay their abilities, whether it's around their career, something they enjoy, or a natural talent. Nobody likes the person who thinks he's better than everyone else, but the truth is you're going to perform at the level you believe you're at. Why do you think Muhammad Ali said he was the greatest before he ever was? If you want better results, start speaking more highly of yourself. Try it today and see how strong it makes you feel.
- **Starve your fears.** Maybe "scary" to you is riding a rollercoaster, or perhaps it's revealing a longtime secret crush on a co-worker. Whatever gets your heart pumping and your blood flowing, do it just once. Breaking down the wall of fear shows us that things aren't usually as difficult or scary as we perceived them to be. When you remove fear, amazing things will happen. It

changes your belief system, and confidence and self-esteem skyrocket.

When you do something that goes against social norms or simply departs from your routine, you experience fun, excitement, an adrenaline rush, and a higher level of self-esteem and self-confidence. You feel bolder—like you could do anything. So go ahead—do something fun or unexpected, and see how good it makes you feel.

FANTASIZE ABOUT THE CRAZIEST STUFF YOU CAN DREAM UP

> I live in two unique worlds, traveling between both with just the opening or closing of my eyes.
> —Richelle E. Goodrich

When I was a kid in school, I was the one who always got in trouble for daydreaming. My mind would wander a million miles away from that classroom. I'm sure it had something to do with my lack of interest in my schoolwork, but it was also because I just like to daydream and think wild and crazy things. The teachers would often ask me a question in the middle of their lessons, and sometimes I was so oblivious I didn't even hear them call on me. It didn't make me feel so good at the time when everyone started laughing, but it's kind of funny looking back on it now.

What wild and crazy things did you envision for yourself as a child?

Remember when you were a kid and you probably had the wildest dreams and fantasies? Maybe you were going to be a professional athlete. Maybe you were going to be president of the United States. Or maybe you had wild fantasies of riding horses, racing cars, being a movie star, going to the moon, or becoming a famous singer. As we grow up, we're taught that fantasies are for little kids and that we should stop wasting our time. We're told that if we're ever going to make something of ourselves, we need to get real and focus on developing skills, going to school, and chasing down a good career. Indeed, maybe there is a time to grow up and take certain things a little more seriously, but to lose that wild, imaginative, fun, creative, playful, and childlike side of your mind would be a shame.

Anyone who tells you to stop dreaming and fantasizing about the wildest things you can think up doesn't know what they are talking about. They need to pull the stick out of their ass.

There are a number of reasons I'm so big on fantasizing…

1. Fantasies are fun.
2. They develop our imagination.
3. They are harmless.

4. They get us thinking bigger.
5. They get us thinking about what can be.
6. They spark us into action.
7. They get us excited about something.
8. They are free.
9. They make us optimistic.
10. They build confidence.

I like to fantasize when I'm feeling down. It helps me feel better. I even like to fantasize when I'm feeling well. I encourage you to fantasize about the biggest, most vivacious things you can imagine. Maybe it's about having money. Maybe it's a romantic thought. Maybe it's becoming something bigger than you are now. Whatever it is, know that it's healthy and perfectly normal at any age to dream wild dreams.

Ask yourself, "What do I *really* want?"

- If I could have anything, what would it be?
- If I could go anywhere, where would that be?
- If I could do it with anyone, who would that be?
- If I had a million dollars, what would I do with it?

This is not a waste of time. This gets you off your ass and gets you thinking.

Maybe daydreaming didn't serve my best interests when I should have been listening to the teachers. Perhaps it eats away at my time when I should be more productive as an adult. For all the ways it might get in

Fantasize about the Craziest Stuff You Can Dream Up

the way, I wouldn't trade it for the world. Neither should you. Keep dreaming!

DON'T WASTE YOUR TIME WITH NEW YEAR'S RESOLUTIONS

> May all your troubles last as long as your New Year's resolutions.
>
> —Joey Adams

It's New Year's Day and already the newsfeed is overflowing with bullshit about making resolutions. The posts essentially say the same crap:

- This is going to be your year!
- It's a fresh start.
- Go after your dreams this year.
- Start attracting greatness into your life.
- You can achieve anything you want.

There's even an event I saw called "The Art of Goal Achieving," where for only a few thousand dollars you can learn how to create even more shitty resolutions that you'll never do anything about.

Let's set the record straight once and for all. I'm all for true goal-setting. I'm all about making positive changes in your life. I'm all for self-improvement. What I'm not all about, however, is bullshit. I pulled that stick out of my ass a long time ago, and so should you.

The problem with New Year's resolutions is that most people are lying to themselves. In fact, they're not just lying; their bullshit meter is off the charts. They're coming up with resolutions because it's the thing to do. Or in some cases, they *think* they want to make a big change, but they don't think about what's really involved to get to their goal. They brainwash themselves into believing that come January 1, all of a sudden something is going to magically change, and things—more specifically, their actions—are going to be drastically different. And you wonder why so many people abandon their goals less than a week into the new year!

Two defining factors for New Year's resolutions…

If you're serious about making and sticking to a New Year's resolution or any other goal, there are two defining factors that must be with you every step of the way.

The first is a true desire to make a change. If you're making a New Year's resolution for fun, or to keep up with your friends who are also doing it, or to play into the hype, forget about it. It's not going to happen. Successfully making a genuine change starts with a real, honest desire to make that change. Without it, you're not going to be successful.

Let's say you set a goal to lose 10 pounds this year. Do you really want to lose 10 pounds or are you just making shit up for the sake of being like everyone else? Why do you want to lose the weight? Is it just because you think it would be fun to do, or deep down do you really have a burning desire to lose it? Unless the goal is something that you really desire with all your heart, it's not going to happen.

Think about any other time you've set a goal and been successful. Your success was a result of wanting it so freaking bad that you did anything and everything to see to it that you accomplished it. Unless you're really serious at that kind of level, cut the crap and pull the stick out of your ass.

The second part to making a successful New Year's resolution is supporting your goal with an effective plan. So many people are making empty promises and spewing bullshit about big things to come in the new year, but they have absolutely no idea how they're going to make it happen. *Puff*—just like that, everything is going to change, but they can't tell you how it's going to happen. In general, I'm more of a "play it by ear" kind of guy, but not when it comes to something you are extremely serious about accomplishing.

Let's say you're dead set on losing those 10 pounds or whatever the number is. It's great to say you're going to do it, but *how* exactly are you going to do it? What is the game plan? What steps are you going to take to lose the weight? What are you going to do differently? Most importantly, what are you going to do when you encounter an obstacle or have an off day? What happens when you're at the bar with your friends and everyone is downing beers and eating fried food? Are you really going to sit there munching on your celery sticks and carrots while they poke fun at you?

One final point about New Year's resolutions or any other goal: you're going to f*ck up, and that's okay. Many people want you to believe it's an all-or-nothing deal. That's just bad advice. Just as most people can't stop smoking cold turkey, you'll more than likely take two steps forward and one step back with your goals. So what if you do? The truth is, making a change is never easy, so simplify the process, go at your own pace, and if you have some mess-ups along the way, that's perfectly okay.

Healthy ways to approach serious goal-setting...

- Avoid the obnoxious self-help gurus with their messages of fluff.

- Stay away from New Year's resolutions unless you are really serious about doing them. Question your motivations behind setting a particular goal to discern your true intentions and whether they are really deriving from your own desires.
- Why wait until January 1? Any day is a good day to go after a goal about which you are serious.
- You must have a plan to support you in achieving your goal.
- You may very well screw up over and over again, but don't get discouraged. Keep pushing forward. If the goal is that important and you're that serious about it, you'll find a way to make it happen in time.

DON'T LET THE QUEST FOR MORE KILL YOU

> Every person needs to take one day away. Jobs, family, employers, and friends can exist one day without any one of us. Each person deserves a day away in which no problems are confronted, no solutions searched for. Each of us needs to withdraw from the cares which will not withdraw from us.
> —Maya Angelou

My phone rang late the other night. It was my friend Michael. He said, "Bruce, I'm in the hospital. I don't know what's wrong. I haven't been sleeping well lately. I can't catch my breath. I'm running on nervous energy. Can you come sit with me?" This hit me right in the gut because I immediately thought he was having a panic attack, something I have experienced more times than I care to remember and that I wouldn't wish on my worst enemy. Turns out, he was just exhausted, dehydrated, stressed to the max, and pushing himself too much.

Michael is a good guy, great family man, and a super hard worker. In fact, his only downfall, if you can call it that, is that he goes above and beyond more than anyone ever should. I always joke with him about his perfectionism, how he can't ever chill out and let things just be. He has a very successful construction business, and he works 17-hour days to make sure that his business is the best it can be.

These kinds of stories are more common than you might realize. I see it all the time with entrepreneurs, people who have phobic personalities, and others who are overachievers. In fact, I've been that person before, lying in a hospital bed chilling out thanks to some high-powered anti-anxiety medication.

For my first real job I worked crazy long hours. I would do the overnight shift three days a week and then a late afternoon into the evening schedule the other two days. Some of the shifts were 12 hours long with no lunch break, and it was very stressful and fast-paced work. I was exhausted and neglected to take care of myself. I was young, stupid, and thought I was invincible. It bit me in the ass when one day my body just shut down. I was given IV fluids in the ER for dehydration and anti-anxiety medication to cool me off, and I was told to go home and rest.

Although I learned a great deal from that experience, I still find myself working odd hours. I own a business and am very involved in the day-to-day operational aspects of it. I'll admit that I have a hard time disconnecting from work. But it's so important! This isn't something you should *try* to do. Putting work down and taking a break is something we all have to do.

Work hard, but play harder.

Working hard is a wonderful attribute. After all, it's what the American Dream was built on. Wanting to be the best is something worthy of striving for. Putting in hours on end is what's often needed to beat out the competition and make it to the top. What's not so great is killing yourself in the process, or at the very least, making yourself sick, be it mentally or physically. I had a hard time pulling this stick out of my ass, and sometimes I still do, but creating a better work-life balance is totally worth it.

Do I still work hard? Hell yeah. Am I still driven and try to beat out others in my industry? Definitely. Do I love to win? All the time. But gone are the days where I will sacrifice my health over it. The "give 110 percent" line is bullshit, in my book. It should be 100 percent and not an ounce more. Whenever I say that, someone always accuses me of being lazy or not really wanting to win. Think again! That's not laziness. That's common sense. After all, what good is all the success in the world; all the clients in the world; all the fame, glory, pride, and money in the world, if you don't have your health to enjoy it?

There are some so-called business gurus who love to say that while your friends are out having fun and relaxing on a Friday night, you should be home focusing on your business. Screw that! That's the worst advice I've ever heard because you need down time to clear your mind, chill out, and take a break from working so hard. Whether it's business-related or something else, the quest for more can cost you your friends, your happiness, your health, and potentially even your life.

I admire people who are driven to want more for themselves. They have this insatiable quest for more that never seems to diminish. But use a little common sense: pull the "I have to do more than I am capable of doing" stick out of your derrière, and make time to enjoy your life.

Don't work hard to enjoy your retirement; enjoy your life now.

We're taught that we have to work at least to the age of 65 in order to do the things we want to do. Screw that. What if you don't make it to 65? I want to enjoy the things I want to do now. I don't mind working hard. I like being successful. I have a desire to do big things. The key is not to kill yourself in the process. Live life and enjoy as much of it as you can now. Below are some strategies for not letting workaholism or the drive for more become a major stick in your ass.

- **Take breaks throughout the day.** I don't care what you do, just get away from your work. Go for a walk, play around online, go for a drive, or do something else that helps you decompress. Your lunch hour doesn't always have to be about eating lunch.
- **Ignore the people who tell you that you have to work all day and all night**, that you can't ever socialize or do things that bring you enjoyment. That's the fast track to burnout.
- **Work hard but play harder**, no matter what your definition of play is.
- **Always use all of your paid time off.** If you let it go unused, that's just stupid. The company will survive without you for a few days.
- **Take a day off to do whatever the hell you want to do once in a while.** A "personal day" can help you reconnect with other parts of yourself other than just your professional self—even if those other parts of yourself just want to sit in a dark room and play Xbox.
- **Know when enough is enough and when to call it a day.** As Anne Lamott writes, "Almost everything will work again if you unplug it for a few minutes, including you."

- **Anything more than 100 percent is bullshit.** Literally—it's not even numerically possible to give more than 100 percent of yourself.
- **Big dreams and wanting more are commendable, but they're never worth sacrificing your physical or emotional health over.** What good is it if you get to where you want to be, only to wind up an emotional or physical wreck?

There's no such thing as perfection.

A lot of people are out chasing perfection or the perfect life. For some, it's a vision of the perfect family living in the perfect house with two perfectly behaved kids and a perfectly painted white picket fence around the perimeter. Others want the perfect vacation, including perfectly cooked meals while relaxing in perfectly styled, Instagram-worthy accommodations and chilling on the perfect white sand beach. Or maybe you're looking for the perfect mate—you know, the one who is a perfect 10 who also has the intelligence and perfect personality to match their good looks.

Unfortunately, there's no such thing as perfection. It's a delusion. Pull the stick out of your ass, and realize it doesn't exist and you're never going to find it. You might come close. You might find something so unbelievably good. But no matter what it is, there will always be some flaw. Guess what? That's perfectly (no pun intended) fine. Maybe a few things in life can be done perfectly, like getting a perfect score on a test, for example, but there's no such thing as the perfect student, the perfect employee, the perfect marriage, the perfect leader, the perfect doctor, or the perfect anything else.

Perfectionism isn't a healthy desire for quality results.

I believe you should always try your best. That's all you can do. Always find ways to improve and learn from your mistakes. But perfectionism isn't a healthy desire for quality results; it's a major stick in the ass. It's time-consuming and will suck the energy right out of you. Striving for perfection is a hallmark of people with anxiety disorders. I know. I chased and chased it for a very long time in almost everything I did. Even when I did something really well of which I should have been proud, I still found a reason—even the most minor detail—to criticize myself, not be satisfied, or try to make it even better. It really sucked!

Maybe for you it's your personal appearance. Maybe you change outfits ten different times until you find the "right" one, only to go back and wear the very first thing you put on. Maybe you sit there and obsess over your hair or makeup. Maybe it's the way you prepare for a get-together or a big presentation. Maybe you clean the house for hours before company comes over. Maybe you reread your e-mails over and over again before you send them. Whatever it is, it's time to pull the stick out and move on.

Again, it's wonderful to strive for great things. It commendable that you want to stand out and make a good impression or be the best you can be. But remember, there's a big difference between being great at something and being a perfectionist.

Don't teach your kids to be perfect either. You're setting them up for disaster and disappointment now and later on in life. Teach them to do the best they can, be the best they can be, make improvements along the way, and understand that if they try their best, that's always good enough. It drives me nuts when parents come down on their kids for not being perfect. When your child comes home with an 85 percent on their test, you should praise the shit out of them. Instead, I know many parents who will practically punish their kids and go off on them for less-than-perfect grades. It's stupid and uncalled for. Stop bullying your kids by having them strive for perfection. You'll make them anxious and stressed out. It's not worth it.

Pull the stick out of your ass and realize there's nothing good or healthy about being a perfectionist. It will eventually bring about the opposite effect of what you're trying to achieve and you'll experience burnout, anxiety, and depression. When you start going into obsessive mode and begin analyzing every little detail, or when you have something to be proud of but you want to make it even better, just stop, put it down, and walk away. Here are some general guidelines for combating the drive for perfection:

- Be the best you can be, and give everything you do your all.
- Know where to draw the line. Recognize the difference between greatness and perfectionism.
- Once you create something awesome, let it be. You've done your job.
- If you start overanalyzing, step back and take a break.
- If you get into an obsessive mode, remember how drained you're going to feel afterward.
- Learn from your mistakes, and always try to better yourself.
- Be proud of your greatness, and stop trying to find flaws.

By implementing these strategies, you will hopefully be able to appreciate yourself for who you are and the quality work you do, rather than comparing your life to unrealistic models. The truth is, even if you want to live a "perfect" life (which doesn't exist), perfectionism will only derail you from the path of success and happiness.

DON'T PUT OTHERS BEFORE YOURSELF

> The number-one priority in life is to take care of yourself and make sure you're happy.
> —Sabrina Carpenter

Life can be crazy. No matter what our age is, we have plenty of responsibilities and tasks to complete. As children, it's about schoolwork, extracurricular activities, and socialization. As adults, it seems like one big balancing act between our career, family life, meeting financial responsibilities, time for friends or hobbies, and so much more.

We've been sold a lie.

On top of that, and adding to the mad rush of life, is the lie we've been sold about putting other people before ourselves. If you're a people pleaser like I tend to be, this can be especially difficult. I enjoy helping other people. I'm not saying you should be intentionally mean or rude to people, but the reality is that you have to put yourself first and take care of number one before you can help numbers two, three, and four.

I was in Boston to give a speech and was on the subway when this chatty woman sat down beside me. I'm not one to make small talk, as you might have guessed. I prefer to keep to myself, especially when on the subway because I enjoy observing how it works. We don't have subways in Florida and I'm always mesmerized by anything transportation related. Nonetheless, I made eye contact with the chatty lady next to me. She said, "You know, sometimes it feels like there's just not enough time in the day." I was having a busy morning myself and just kind of nodded in agreement. During that 15-minute train ride, she went on to talk about being a single mom to three girls all while juggling a busy career as a tech executive. Her days had her up at 5:00 A.M., making breakfast, getting her daughters fed and ready for school, fighting the morning commute to make it to work by 9:00 A.M., taking part in meetings throughout the day and being under tight deadlines, all to get home by 5:00 P.M. to make dinner, help her girls with their homework, get them ready for bed, and then repeat it all the next day. I was tired just from listening to her story.

The thing that I found most remarkable is that for all the craziness this woman was dealing with, she was very calm, collected, put-together, and seemed to have it all under control. I asked her how she did it without letting it all get to her. She said, "I always make time for myself every single day of the year no matter what is going on."

We're aware that self-care is important, but we never make time for ourselves.

Making time for myself was something I was never really good at. I was always doing things for other people, but I was neglecting myself. The day I pulled that self-neglect stick out of my ass and started carving out time for myself was life-changing. Now making time for myself is something I do every single day, and you should, too.

When you tell people they need to make time for themselves, most of them will nod in agreement but never really do anything about it. Or they'll come back at you with a million excuses about why they're too busy. The thing is, I'm not talking about five or six hours out of your day. Even taking just 20 to 30 minutes each day to focus on yourself can do wonders for your mental and physical health. Hell, if that's asking too much, just take five minutes.

Nobody likes a martyr.

The reality is you cannot give so much of yourself to help other people until you are making it a priority to take care of yourself first. What's that idiom about pouring from an empty cup? In fact, I'd go so far as to say that the most selfish thing you can do is to continually place your own needs on the backburner, because doing so will negatively impact your ability to contribute and your attitude about doing so.

Never making time for yourself can cause burnout, resentment, and bitterness. Below are some strategies for avoiding martyrdom and implementing a practice of self-care.

- **Stop overextending yourself, and start putting yourself first.** You can't do everything, and even if you could, you'd be a miserable wreck, totally unable to enjoy the fruits of your labor.
- **Find the time for self-care.** It can be on your lunch break, after the kids go to bed, before you leave for work in the morning, or whenever it's convenient for you. When you do it doesn't matter. Just find the time to do something for yourself every single day, no matter what.
- **Do something enjoyable.** Maybe it's reading a book; sitting on a park bench people watching; listening to music; playing golf; painting; sitting in a coffee shop, playing chess; writing a letter or journaling; taking a long hot shower or bath; or lying in your bed, staring at the ceiling, and doing absolutely nothing at all but talking to yourself. Whatever is going to help you

disconnect and get away from the world; relax, refresh, and recharge; and just make you forget about any responsibilities and stress, is what you want to do.
- **Silence external noise.** This is your time and that means no outside interruptions. No smartphones, laptops, or tablets. No kids. No spouse. No parents. No friends. Nothing and no one but you.
- **Focus on your physical body.** If you're feeling overly stressed and on edge, do something that will relax you. Sometimes that can mean getting active to release it all, and other times that can mean trying to lie still and perform breathing exercises. If your current needs call for quiet relaxation, try reflecting on the silence or putting on some music that relaxes you. Iron Maiden might not do it. Concentrate on slowing your breathing. Breath in through your stomach area, hold for a few seconds, and slowly breathe out through your lips. You can also try relaxation recordings or muscle relaxation techniques, both of which are great for relieving tension.

DON'T RUSH TO THE GRAVE

> I spent my whole childhood wishing I were older and now I'm spending my adulthood wishing I were younger.
>
> —Ricky Schroder

When I was a kid, all I wanted to do was be able to drive a car. I can clearly remember the day I turned 15 and got my learner's permit. I was so excited. I went out driving that night with my dad. What a thrill.

The allure of adulthood is strong.

When I was in college, I wished I could be 21 so I could buy alcohol legally. My friends thought I looked the oldest of us all, and every Friday night I would dress up in nice clothes, put on my glasses, and not shave for a few days so I looked even older. I would go to the store to try to buy alcohol. Funny thing is, most of the time I got away with it. My friends loved me for it.

Growing up I wanted to be a television news reporter. I rushed my way through college, got an internship in my sophomore year of school, and had more real-life experience than anyone else my age and got hired before any of my friends.

It's funny looking back because I had such a stick in my ass and was in such a rush to become an adult. My thinking was, "Everything is going to be better when I get a little older." Not that anything was wrong or I didn't like being a kid, but the allure of growing up and being an adult, having unlimited freedom and independence, was so strong.

Guess what? I was wrong! Maybe it was a case of "the grass is greener on the other side." Maybe it was just wanting what I couldn't have. Whatever it was, it was stupid.

Are there some perks to being an adult? Hell yeah. Now I can drive whenever I want. I can also buy alcohol legally whenever I want, not that I really do all that much. There are a lot of things I can do. There's something I can't do, though: be a kid again.

Enjoy whatever stage you're currently in.

So many people are in a hurry to get through something and come out on the other side. They're

- rushing through primary and secondary school to get to college;

- rushing through college to get to their career;
- rushing through the week to get to the weekend;
- rushing through the month to make it to the next payday;
- rushing through dating to get to marriage;
- rushing through the newborn phase, toddler phase, etc., to get to a less frenzied state of parenting;
- and rushing through their career to get to retirement.

Phew, I'm stressed just reading that list!

The problem is, what is the other side of these things? Once you're done with school, sure, you might get a paycheck, but you never have a long eight-week summer break to look forward to again. When you're counting down the weekdays to get to the weekend, the days of one month to get to another, the final months until a new year, before you know it another year has passed you by and you've lost the joys of experiencing it.

When you focus on your children growing up instead of being present with them during the time when you are their whole world, all of a sudden they will be grown up and won't want to spend as much time with you. Those are years you can never get back. There's a reason people say about childrearing, "The days are long but the years are short."

With all these things, it's like people are checking off boxes to ensure they've hit all the to-do's in life. Married?

PULL THE STICK OUT OF YOUR @$$

Check. Bought our first house? *Check.* Had a baby? *Check.* Put the kids through college? *Check.* You get the idea. But after you check off all the boxes, what's left? That's right—the grave. It's not a pleasant thought.

So stop looking forward to the next phase of your life, whatever that might be, and focus on enjoying the one you're currently in. Remember, you'll never get today back (unless they invent time travel, in which case... watch out 1994). Every moment truly is a gift, and working to be present in and grateful for each one will help you pull any stick out of your ass and find peace in the here and now instead of the hereafter.

DON'T SHIT ON YOURSELF

> I seek strength, not to be greater than others, but to fight my greatest enemy, the doubts within myself.
> —P. C. Cast

Why is it that we're so quick to eliminate the physical waste from our bodies, but when it comes to our mental shit, some of us just poop all over ourselves? I used to take a mental dump on myself all the time. Occasionally, I still do, but I'm getting better at finding ways to eliminate my psychological waste in more effective ways.

There are a lot of ways that people shit on themselves, but I want to tell you about three phrases in particular that you may be using without being aware of the damage they're doing. These words are the worst of any.

"I should have…"

One of the most common phrases among people who suffer from self-doubt is "I should have." Almost every action they take is immediately followed by the words "I should have done this" or "I should have done that." It's the ultimate form of self-defeat. Therapists tell their patients not to "should on themselves." I say "don't shit on yourself" because really, that's what it is.

There are times when you really screw something up, and it would certainly be appropriate to say, "I should have done..." But the truth is, most of the time, whatever we set out to accomplish we usually did just fine. It's our own ridiculously outrageous standards we set for ourselves that make us question our own abilities. And if we do mess something up, that's okay too. As Theodore Roosevelt said, "The only man who never makes a mistake is the man who never does anything."

Sometimes our doubt is a result of wanting to look good and impress those around us. Even if someone was watching, they probably weren't paying attention to the point of scrutinizing every detail, because they were too into whatever they were doing. Whether or not someone noticed, it doesn't help to beat yourself up over the changes you could've made to your approach. And more times than not, if you're not proud of the results of your actions, you can get a do-over and try again.

We all have mess-ups in our lives. Sometimes it's more than just an error at work; sometimes we screw things up in a relationship. Things get heated, our emotions get the best of us, stress becomes overwhelming, and we act and speak without thinking first. Other times, we're just outright stupid and do things that aren't really a representation of who we really are. It could be a way of acting out, trying to fit in, getting people to notice us, moving past painful experiences, the result of being angry, or just a bad spur-of-the-moment decision.

Even to this day, I still do stupid shit all the time. Hopefully my mistakes aren't the type that hurt people or are deliberate. Hopefully my errors continue to get smaller and less significant as the years go by.

When they do happen, though, I do my best to learn from them so I can be a better person in the future. I quickly apologize to anyone I may have hurt as a result of my actions. Then, I make peace with what I have done and let it go.

It might sound strange since, after all, you were the jerk who did the hurting, but at some point, once you apologize and it really sinks in what you did, you have to forgive yourself and move on with your life. This doesn't mean you should ever be happy or feel good about what you did, but it does mean you need to realize that we all make mistakes; pull the "I hurt you," "I screwed up," and "I should have" sticks out of your ass; and move on.

Like many of the ideas to make you a stronger, more confident person, eliminating the "should haves" takes a lot of work and patience. When you catch yourself starting a sentence out with "I should have," put that phrase in its place and tell it to f*ck off.

For example: "Damn it. I should have..." The rebuttal is "No! Eff that. I did it just fine." Or for those more egregious mistakes: "Screw this perpetual self-blame; I've apologized and everyone's moved on."

"What if..."

While we're talking about shitting on yourself, the sibling to "I should have" is "what if."

If ever there was one phrase that will send you into a mental frenzy and bring on more physiological symptoms, this is it. It's a never-ending spiral that will drive you absolutely crazy.

What if this happens? What if I die? What if I faint? What if I lose control? What if I make a fool of myself? What if everyone laughs at me? What if I turn red? What if I forget my lines? What if I look nervous? It goes on and on and on.

Believe it or not, your brain is simply trying to protect you by pointing out the worst-case scenario. Of course, this part of the brain isn't logical enough to realize that the worst case seldom happens.

Just as you must handle the "should haves," putting the "what ifs" in their place is equally important. One great strategy is replacing a "what if" with a "so what if" and then answering the question realistically.

- @ What if I feel nervous?
- − So what if I feel nervous? I'll find a quiet place to calm down, and it will pass in a few minutes.
- @ What if I can't do it?
- − So what if I can't do it? I need to at least try. If I still can't do it, no big deal; I'll try another time.
- @ What if I lose my job?
- − So what if I lose my job? I have a lot of great skills and experience, and I'll find another job or start my own company.

Perhaps the ultimate "what if" rebuttal is: *What if I'm six feet underground and I let fear make me miss out on an amazing opportunity?* That should get you moving.

"I can't…"

There's one more sibling to "I should have" and "what if." Her name is "I can't." Holy crap, I hate this one because I fought it for years.

I can't do it. I can't do the job because I'm not qualified. I can't get on the plane because I'll freak out and have a panic attack. I can't ask the girl out because she's out of my league. I can't support myself because I got bad grades in school.

Similar to "I should have," you have to tell "I can't" to get lost as well. Perhaps in the theoretical sense there are some things I really can't do. I can't walk on water. I can't fly myself to the moon. I can't eat an apple and shit a fruit salad. But with most endeavors, "I can't" is just another instance of my mind trying to play tricks on me and consuming me with self-doubt, which it can try to do...but I'm going to push back.

Pay attention to the symptoms of self-doubt.

There will be days when despite your best efforts to eliminate these words and all your insecurities and self-doubts, you won't be able to. Sometimes this will happen when you least expect it; and in fact, it's those days when you're running on cruise control that you're more likely to get a great big self-doubt stick shoved up your ass. Be prepared and watch the language you use with yourself and others. When you catch yourself using the three phrases mentioned above, or other self-destructive ones, don't drown yourself in a pool of self-pity and dwell on it. That would be perpetuating the toxic cycle of self-limiting beliefs!

Pay very close attention to those thoughts that creep into the back of your mind. Sometimes you won't even be able to identify the thoughts; you'll just feel defeated. The moment you experience any symptoms of this self-doubt manifesting, be ready to confront it head on by telling it to get lost because it's not welcomed at the party.

TO HELL WITH CONFORMITY— BE WHO YOU REALLY ARE

> Remember always that you not only have the right to be an individual, you have an obligation to be one.
> —Eleanor Roosevelt

Mark Zuckerberg doesn't look like a guy who's worth $53.7 billion wearing his T-shirt, hoodie, and jeans. John Daly doesn't look like your typical professional golfer with his beer belly hanging out, his nontraditional golf swing, and his "grip it and rip it" motto. Marilyn Manson isn't exactly Barry Manilow in his appearance or vocals. All of these people are nonconformists whose differences have not limited their success; if anything, their originality has magnified their achievements. Not only are these individuals extremely successful, but they also have the freedom of not really caring about what anyone thinks of them or their differences.

Nonconformity signals confidence and contentment with who you really are.

It reminds me of how there's always that one guy in a professional setting sporting ripped jeans, a T-shirt, and blue hair. Corporate recruiters would steer clear of him at all costs, but I know he's someone not to be ignored. Why? He doesn't have a stick up his ass and isn't worried about what other people think, which means he's got confidence and a true appreciation of who he really is. He knows exactly what works for him, and he's successful enough that he doesn't need to care what others think of his fashion choices.

You might find this surprising based on things I have revealed about my own personality, but I like myself a lot. I'm not saying that in a cocky way like, "Hey, look at me," or "I'm so good." That's not what I mean at all. I just like the person I am. I've always liked myself. Sure, there are times when I wish I was different in many ways. For example, it would be great to be more outgoing. It would have been nice to have been less anxious about things growing up. It would be really great to have a better short game on the golf course. There are plenty of moments I would take back and things I would do differently. However, for the most part, I'm really content with the person I am. I wouldn't change much at all about myself, despite some of my differences and quirks.

You have to be your own biggest fan.

I really believe this is where it all begins: You have to like who you are. You have to be your biggest fan. You have to look in the mirror and be like, "Damn, look at me. I look good, and I like myself." (This gets more difficult when your hair is turning gray and falling out.) You have to be the one who comforts yourself during tough times. You have to fight for yourself, because nobody else will. It all starts with your belief in *you*. Maybe that sounds like a bunch of motivational bullshit, but it's true.

When I was in high school, Z. Cavaricci pants were the big thing. (Yeah, I'm old.) As *Complex Magazine* said, "That little white tab on the front of the fly meant you were hip." Everyone was wearing them. Everyone except me. I didn't like them. I thought they looked goofy. I was the only one. I was in the mall one time with some friends, and they made me try a pair on. I still didn't like them. My parents even offered to get them for me, but I said no. As someone who, at the time, was plagued by what other people thought and always wanted to conform to societal norms, it's surprising I didn't go with the trend. For some reason, I wanted to be different. I wanted to wear my grungy T-shirts and shorts. I liked who I really was, and that was the most important thing to me, even if other people didn't approve and I wasn't the most popular guy in my class.

The truth is, there are plenty of people who are, well, like plenty of other people. What's so great about that? But if you're not a shirt-and-tie kind of guy or don't have clean-cut hair parted to the side, good for you. Be different. Be you. Be proud. Don't worry about what other people think of your nonconformist ways. If they don't like it, they need to pull the stick out of their ass. It's not your problem. It's theirs. Screw conformity. Be who you really are meant to be.

You can't reinvent yourself.

I was reading a personal development book by a well-known self-help author recently, and the chapter was about reinventing yourself. "WTF?" I asked myself. "Reinvent yourself? What the hell does that mean?" Let's be perfectly clear about something: there's no such thing as reinventing yourself. You're not a car being reintroduced as a new model. You're not a next-generation computer that was improved from an existing model. There is only one you. You're not going into the factory and being cloned or reinvented.

Of course, I know what the author was getting at. He was talking about making changes and new choices in your life to better yourself. Then just say, "Here are some ways to make changes in your life" or "Here are some things you can do differently." Don't say, "Reinvent yourself." That's scary sounding.

Kidding aside, I really believe that reinventing yourself, by most people's definition, is impossible and even stupid. Can you make changes in your life? Sure. Can you learn to do things differently? Of course. Can you overcome your fears and phobias? Absolutely. Can you learn new skills to make yourself emotionally stronger? You bet. The reason I don't like to call it a "reinvention" is simply because you are special. There is only one of you, and you are uniquely talented in your own special and specific ways. I don't like the idea of a reinvention because the truth is, even the characteristics, behaviors, and habits that we don't necessarily like are a part of who we are. As much as they can be a major stick in the ass, they are a part of the "real" us, and they do serve an important purpose.

There are upsides to even negative experiences. For example, my social phobia makes me a better listener, and my panic attacks made me more observant. While I do want to minimize my phobic behaviors, the reality is they have served me well in many other aspects of my life. The skills I have learned as a result of some of the things I don't like about myself have been eye-opening and life-changing.

If you don't like your clothing, maybe you can have a wardrobe reinvention. If you don't like your hairstyle, maybe you can have a hairdo reinvention. When it comes to who you are, what you're made of, what separates you from the crowd, and what makes you special, the fact is there is nothing to reinvent. Focus on minimizing certain behaviors you dislike while really trying to enhance the ones that are already working for you. But never change the person you really are. That's just stupid and misguided advice. You're you, and there's only one of you—and that person is already awesome.

Strategies for embracing your true, weird-ass self...

- **Accept your differences.** Be proud of who you are and what you like. Never think about changing your interests because they're not what most people like.
- **Be respectful of other people's interests.** I might not care about NCAA sports, your music, or playing cards, but I respect the fact that you do.
- **Be open-minded about trying other people's interests.** Always be willing to sample that food that your friend really enjoys or go to that concert that your best friend wants you to go with him to. Maybe you'll like it, and maybe you won't. Either way, be willing to try it. It's okay to be different, but it's unacceptable to be closed-minded.
- **Don't take crap from anyone over who you are or what you like.** If they don't like what you're into, it's not your problem.

- **Real friends have many things in common, but they also have their share of differences.** I have a few close friends, and we see eye to eye on some things but are worlds apart on others. That's okay.
- **Laugh it off.** People can't make fun of you if you're already making fun of yourself. This strategy is so crucial that it's the focus of the next chapter.

LAUGH AT YOURSELF— IT'S THE KEY TO DISARMING OTHERS

> I don't get embarrassed easily, and I do silly things all the time!
>
> —Emily Osment

I was sitting at the table with my son eating breakfast. As I'm biting into my Cheerios, he lets out a really big fart. I mean, it was a loud one. In that moment, I realized I had an opportunity to teach him a very important lesson about how to handle an embarrassing situation.

As I see it, he had two choices for how to react:

1. He could have been embarrassed and run off in shame, not feeling very good about himself.
2. He could laugh it off and we would go about eating our breakfast.

I knew my reaction would determine what he did, so naturally, I chose option number two. I looked at him and started laughing and said, "That was a good one!" Then he started laughing and everything was okay. You can't always control your bodily functions, but you can control how you handle any awkwardness that results.

I know this from personal experience. When I was in ninth grade, I was sitting in English class with a really bad cold one day. My nose was dripping like crazy, and I was constantly wiping it. Some rude kid screamed out, "Look at Bruce. He's picking his nose!" I was mortified. After all, I was sick, felt like crap, and didn't need this punk calling me out in front of the whole class.

I remember this story like it was yesterday because of my reaction. Back then, I had a major stick up my ass, and I didn't know how to go with the flow and laugh at myself. If I knew then what I know now, this would have been a very meaningless moment in my life that I would not still remember almost 30 years later.

Embarrassing moments happen to all of us. The thing to realize is that the embarrassing situation usually isn't as bad as you think it is. It is your reaction that gives it power. It is your reaction that gives other people power. If you let it get to you, it will. But if you can accept it and laugh at it, then it has no power. In fact, if you can bring attention to it and laugh it off in front of others, you've just taken the power away from them making a big thing of it, too.

Laugh at Yourself—It's the Key to Disarming Others

Imagine if, when I was back in ninth grade, I had run with it when that kid called me out in front of the class. I should have laughed. I should have said, "Ha ha, look at me. I'm a nose picker." I would have taken away any power that he or any of my other classmates had to make a bad situation worse.

I am hopeful that I taught my son a very important lesson at the breakfast table. I hope that I taught him not to have a stick up his ass when something embarrassing happens and to just go with it and laugh. Hopefully, when he does something embarrassing when he's with his friends or in a professional setting one day, he will remember this and easily be able to work through it.

I do all sorts of embarrassing things every single day. Sure, sometimes I'm not exactly all that impressed with my goofs, but if I let them eat away at me I'd be in really bad shape. My stress and anxiety from it would be sucking the joy out of my life if I didn't know how to handle it. So instead, I have learned to pull the stick out of my ass, just laugh it off, and go with it. Let me tell you, it's been one of the greatest things I ever learned to do.

FOLLOW YOUR HEART AND EVERYTHING ELSE JUST FOLLOWS

> Do what you love; you'll be better at it. It sounds pretty simple, but you'd be surprised how many people don't get this one right away.
>
> —LL Cool J

I'll never forget reading an online advertisement for a new start-up airline called JetBlue that had just launched service between Fort Lauderdale and New York City. It was the year 2001. They needed ramp agents. I wasn't working at the time, and at first glance I thought about applying but quickly decided it was probably best to stick to something more in line with my intended career path. Later in the afternoon, I started thinking about applying for the job some more and ultimately decided to do it. I thought, *What the* hell? *If they get back to me and it goes somewhere, that could be fun. And if it doesn't, that's okay, too.*

It's amazing the difference in how you feel when you're doing something you love.

I've already talked about how much I love airplanes, and in part two of the book I'm going to tell you how I overcame my flying phobia. As you know, aviation is something very close to my heart. I thought it might be good to explore a job in something I really love. Sure enough, I got a phone call a few days later inviting me for an interview. It went great, and I got the job.

I went through a few weeks of training and for the next six months worked full-time in ground operations, loading and unloading airplanes; wing walking; marshalling the planes to their parking positions; pushing them off the gate; sitting in the flight deck, going over the weight and balance of the aircraft with the pilots; and getting to see the inner workings of how an airline runs. It was one of the coolest experiences of my life, but unfortunately the physical labor took a toll on me and I developed terrible tendinitis.

More important than the enjoyment of those six months was the bigger life lesson I learned: pull the stick out of your ass, and do what you love. I don't know about you, but for me, any time I do something because I *have* to do it compared to something I *want* to do, it's a major difference in how I feel. When I'm doing the things I love, I'm genuinely happy, fulfilled, and satisfied. My overall well-being is in a much better state. When I'm doing things that I don't necessarily care for but have to do, I'm usually doing it half-assed—just going through the motions and feeling relatively unfulfilled. This does nothing for my mental well-being. In fact, it can even adversely affect it.

If you're going to spend eight hours a day working, it might as well be in a job you enjoy.

I totally get that sometimes we have to do things we don't want to do. I don't like to do laundry. I never really liked school. I don't like driving four hours to go visit family. I'm not talking about the must-haves in life that you just have to bite your tongue and do. I'm talking about things like your career and pastimes. If you're going to spend eight hours a day working, it might as well be in a job that you genuinely enjoy. Sure, there are times when you have to make money and do some things that you see as less desirable, but generally speaking, just do the things you really want to do. It's not only more fun this way, but you're going to feel more connected and excited, have less anxiety and depression, and just feel a lot better about yourself and life as a whole. The other thing—your level of happiness and fulfillment will trickle over into everything else in your life. When I was around airplanes all the time, people thought I was taking drugs because I was a different person.

Are you worried about what other people will think? Guess what? Screw them! This is not their life. It's yours. Pull the stick out of your ass, because it's not your job to make them happy. You have to be happy. I had my share of people who were left perplexed about why I was working for an airline. "Don't you want to be a TV reporter?" they would ask. "Shouldn't you be working a job that requires a college degree?" others would say. I didn't care. It wasn't their business. It was a real job. It was legal and legitimate work. Most importantly, I was the happiest I had ever been.

What are the things that you enjoy the most? Go after them with everything you've got, and I promise you'll never once look back or have any regrets.

DON'T QUIT YOUR DAY JOB

> Entrepreneurship is throwing yourself off a cliff and building a plane on the way down.
> —Reid Hoffman

- You can become a millionaire!
- You can have immense freedom and do what you want whenever you want!
- You can call all the shots!
- Stop building someone else's dream and start building yours!

Sounds pretty glamourous, doesn't it? If only it were that easy. Like most things in life, if it sounds too good to be true, it probably is. I know I just spent the last chapter telling you to go after what it is in life that truly ignites your passion, but there's one caveat to that...

Think twice before becoming an entrepreneur.

I've been an entrepreneur for almost 10 years, and it's about time someone tells the truth and cuts through all the bullshit—the same nonsense that has led so many people to chase a non-existent dream, go hundreds of thousands of dollars into debt, and suffer from major stress, depression, and anxiety.

There are a million different books, articles, and business gurus out there telling you that owning a business is the greatest thing since sliced bread, the fastest way to become wealthy, and the ultimate form of freedom. To that I say bullshit. For some, it is. However, it's a very tiny minority. In fact, if you take a look at the statistics on small business success, they're pretty daunting. There are different numbers out there, but one report I read recently said that 8 out of 10 entrepreneurs who start a business fail within the first 18 months.

Now this probably seems really strange coming from someone who has his own business and strongly believes in building something for yourself. My point is not to discourage you or talk you out of becoming an entrepreneur but rather to make you aware of what you are really getting into, because there is just so much misinformation out there. After all, pulling the stick out of your ass means being honest, looking out for your best interests, and taking care of your mental and physical health.

Let's cut through the crap and dispel a few myths about starting your own business.

- **You'll make a lot of money.** You might. A lot of businessowners have made a lot. I have at times. But remember, every Friday isn't a guaranteed payday. You can very easily lose a lot of money. I've been here, too. Let me tell you, it's the worst feeling in the world when you have no money coming in, can't pay your bills, can't do fun things, owe people money, etc.
- **It'll give you freedom.** Yes and no. More like, it'll give you flexibility. It's nice when you have to schedule a doctor's appointment in the middle of the day or you have to drive the kids to school. But is freedom being on the phone at 10:00 P.M. with a client who has a problem? Is freedom being on vacation and having to step away from your family to take care of a work issue? Is freedom working 16-hour days and weekends to ensure the success of your business? Is freedom being so stressed out that you have trouble coping and turn to drinking, pills, or develop mental health problems? Hopefully it doesn't come to this for you, but it's important to think of the very serious toll that entrepreneurship can take on your life.
- **It's easy.** Is it easy having to do your job, be the bookkeeper, be the sales department, the janitor,

and worry about everything else in between? Is it easy giving a client bad news? Is it easy when you really mess something up and have no one to turn to?

The truth is, I have days where I absolutely love running my own business. I have days where I make great things happen for my clients. I have days where, again, the money is good. I also have plenty of days where I just want to walk away from it all and go work for someone else, not have to take the job home with me at night, have a steadier income, and not have to feel as stressed out as I sometimes do from it all.

If you have a great product or service and feel like becoming an entrepreneur is your calling, then go for it. I'm not telling you that if your dream is to own your own business, then you should give that up for something more "practical." What I am saying is to pull the stick out of your ass and be realistic with your expectations. Make sure to put in perspective what other people say about the perks that come with starting a business. Take the rose-colored glasses off, because it's not as glamourous as many people want you to believe.

ENVY CAN BE YOUR BEST FRIEND IF YOU USE IT RIGHT

> Nothing sharpens sight like envy.
> —Thomas Fuller

Every December, my family and I drive around town each night going through the different neighborhoods to see the Christmas lights. A few years ago, I got very down on myself one night while we were doing this. We were driving in this part of town that had these really big, beautiful mansions. Before I knew what happened, I felt a big fat envy stick in my ass. I was beating myself up: *Why can't I have a house like that? Who the hell has that kind of money to afford something like that? Why do I make so little money?* I was mad. I was upset. I felt like a big loser.

My "ah-ha" moment

Later that evening it hit me: I was going about this all wrong. Instead of falling victim to envy, I needed to use it to my advantage to help me get the things I want in life. It was an "ah-ha" moment for me. Now whenever I see something that is out of my reach, I may still get upset at first, but I quickly pull that envy stick out of my ass and use it to work for me rather than against me.

It's funny to me how the word *envy* is used mostly in a negative way. Most psychologists will tell you that envy is bad and should be avoided at all costs, and that true happiness starts from within. I agree that happiness starts with you. I disagree, though, that envy is a bad thing. I think it can be a great motivating force in one's life, just as I now use it in mine. It really comes down to what you do with it.

The reason society looks down on envy is because most people become absorbed in what other people have and even more obsessed with what they *don't* have. Sure, that makes sense, but something really extraordinary happens when you see someone with something you want but that you can't have at that moment: it motivates you to find a way to get it. And that is the beauty of envy.

Don't let envy get you down; let it fire you up.

Let's say your friend is pretty successful and comes riding down the block in a brand-new Ferrari 488 Pista. (Why not go big!) Your first reaction is probably going to be: *Holy shit! What a cool car. I want one.* Now you have a choice: you can fall into a depression and start beating yourself up. This is what most people do when they succumb to the envy trap, and it's why envy gets such a bad rap in society. Most people become consumed with thoughts like: *I suck. I'll never be able to afford one of those. Why am I such a loser? Why can't I be more successful? Man, he has it all. I have $20,000 of credit card debt so how the hell am I ever going to be able to afford a car like that?*

Now, imagine if instead of using your envy to beat yourself up, you used it to move yourself closer to actually acquiring that Ferrari 488 Pista? Now, for the record, most people can't afford that car, which has a starting price tag of about $350,000. But maybe it's not the Ferrari; after all, envy isn't always connected to high-ticket items. Maybe it's a new computer or something more realistic like that. Instead of beating yourself up and coming up with every reason why you suck and why he is better than you, use it to light a fire under your ass to get what you want.

Your thinking could go something like: *I really want that MacBook Pro like Sean just got. I can't afford it* just yet, but that doesn't mean I won't be able to soon. I'll work some more hours or take on some new clients. I'll do what I need to, because man, I want that laptop.

Ask yourself: "What steps do I need to take to acquire or accomplish this?"

Again, the key is to turn your envy and jealousy into a positive action. In fact, don't get depressed because someone has what you want and can't currently get. Ask yourself: *How am I going to acquire this? What do I need to do? What steps can I take to move closer to being able to afford or accomplish this?*

It doesn't have to be a material possession, either. Maybe your best friend has a smoking hot girlfriend or boyfriend who is also really smart and super nice, and your love life is anything but red-hot right now. You can be jealous of them or you can get off your ass and do something about it. Maybe you need to clean yourself up, get a haircut and shave, buy some new clothes, start trying to meet people in different places, and become more confident in who you are. Take the steps you need to move closer to your dreams.

Envy can be the greatest tool for getting what you want in life. The key is not to fall into the trap of jealousy and depression but rather to use envy as motivation to get what you want. The object of desire can be anything: more money, a better job, a nicer car, an advanced degree, more friends, or whatever. Envy is a natural feeling that we all experience. Instead of letting it get you down, make the choice to pull the stick out of your ass and use it to your advantage to get what you really want out of life.

GET OVER YOUR FOMO BECAUSE THE PARTY IS ALWAYS WHERE YOU ARE

> FOMO is the enemy of valuing your own time.
> —Andrew Yang

When I was growing up, I was never invited to the cool parties. Okay, who am I kidding? I wasn't even invited to the not-so-cool parties. But that was okay with me because I really didn't care. Being popular wasn't high up on my priority list. I had my own likes and interests, a few close friends, and I was happy with who I was... most of the time. Occasionally, however, I did question if maybe I was missing out on something. What do the cool kids do? What is a party really like? Where do they all hang out? Am I missing anything fun and exciting?

The only thing that matters is enjoying what *you're* doing.

I attended plenty of parties during college, and while they were a good time and all, I realized I never was really missing out on anything at all by not being part of the in-crowd during high school. What I really learned, and something that holds so true for me to this day, is that the party is always where I am. I don't mean that like "Hey, look how cool I am. It's not a party unless I'm there." I mean that it doesn't matter what other people are off doing because the only thing that matters is enjoying what *I'm* doing.

FOMO = the fear of missing out.

So maybe not being part of the cool crowd didn't faze me much, but there have been plenty of times I felt like I was missing out on things. FOMO (the fear of missing out) is a really big stick in the ass for so many people these days, especially because of social media. We see our friends updating their statuses and uploading pictures of all the fun and cool things they are doing, and we begin to feel isolated, hurt, and jealous. We become consumed with negative thoughts, wondering why we don't have fun like they do, why we don't have the sports car or new set of golf clubs that they have, why they were at a party and we weren't invited, and other things that are missing from our lives.

FOMO is a self-inflicted form of anxiety and unhappiness, but you can learn to get past it. The following techniques will help you feel less concerned about what others are doing and having so that you can be more present and able to enjoy whatever your life happens to look like at the moment.

- **Get real with yourself.** The first step is simple: pull the stick out of your ass and stop worrying about what everyone else is doing. It only matters what *you* are doing. It may sting a bit if you find out some of your friends got together without you or that someone you know went to a concert that you couldn't go to, but tell yourself that it's okay you weren't there. There will be plenty of times that you have opportunities to do things that other people won't get to do.
- **Recognize that you realistically can't do it all.** Remember, you are only one person and you can't be everywhere, with everybody, doing everything all of the time. Stop trying to do it all and spreading yourself thin. There are only 24 hours in a day, so put an emphasis on the quality of the experiences you do have. If you can't do something now, maybe it's something you can do at another time in the future.
- **Remember that most people's social media posts are generally bullshit.** When was the last time you read someone's post on Facebook that said, "My life sucks. I'm feeling so depressed. I

have no friends. I hate myself. I'm in so much emotional pain"? It's extremely rare because most people only post about the good things going on in their life. In other words, everything you see and read about is a very skewed picture of what life is really like for people. Everyone—and I mean everyone—has their share of problems and tough times, just like you. Don't buy into everything you see on social media. Limit your time on social media each day.

- **Focus more on you.** It's good to have friends, but be more concerned with your own life and priorities above anyone else's. Focus on your own happiness, satisfaction, and fulfillment. Take more of a liking to who you really are and focus more on the things you want to do. The more you do this, the less you will care about or get worked up over what other people are doing.

WHEN LIFE THROWS YOU LEMONS, JUST SAY "SCREW IT"

> I believe when life gives you lemons, you should make lemonade...and try to find someone whose life has given them vodka, and have a party.
> —Ron White

I was having a really shitty day, literally. My son had a diaper bomb—you know, one of those times when the diaper just can't hold it all in anymore and poop starts flying everywhere. Everything that could be going wrong was going wrong. The car needed new tires. The A/C system was on the fritz. It was one thing after another.

When things like this happen, it's easy to get caught up in the moment, lose your cool, get mad, and send your stress levels through the roof. We've all done it, and hey, it's a normal reaction when life decides to shit all over you. But instead of letting it get the best of you, sometimes it just feels so good to pull the stick out of your ass and say, "Screw it!" But what does that really mean?

How should you respond to a bad day?

Right now, there are basically two well-established schools of thought on what to do when you're having a really bad day:

1. You can let it consume the hell out of you and ruin the rest of your day, like I described above.
2. You can try to do something about it: fight back, find a solution, or use it as motivation to move forward.

I'd like to introduce a third idea: just say, "Screw it." Saying "screw it" is neither letting it consume you nor trying to do something about it. It's simply just letting it be, but it just sounds better to say "screw it." When you say, "Screw it," something wonderful happens. Whatever "it" is loses all power. It just goes away. There's no feeling bad. There's no ruining your day. There's no being in a bad mood. There's no trying to figure something out. It's neither good nor bad. It's just done. Just say, "Screw it," and go about your business.

Say, "Screw it."
Let it go. Problem solved.

I was having a bad month. Business was a little slow. The bills were piling up. Sure, at first I wanted to react with anger. I wanted to play the blame game. I wanted to puff and complain. Then the optimistic people tried to offer their positive-thinking wisdom: "Fight back," "Don't let it get you down," "You can do this." I wasn't in the mood to hear it. So instead, I chose option number three. I said, "Screw it." I didn't give it power, negative or positive. I just let it be. I let it go, and it was done. Problem solved. I felt better.

Whatever crap life throws your way—and rest assured that crap will in fact get thrown your way—there are of course times when you have to address it with proper action. But sometimes saying, "Screw it" is the correct response and the best thing you can do for yourself and your sanity.

STOP ASKING WHY

> Just knowing you don't have the answers is a recipe for humility, openness, acceptance, forgiveness, and an eagerness to learn—and those are all good things.
> —Dick Van Dyke

I'm an inquisitive person by nature. When something happens, I want to know why. Many times, it's really important to know why. If my children are struggling in school, I need to know why that is so I can figure out how to help them succeed. If I'm constantly tired all the time, my doctor might need to run some tests to figure out why that is so we can address the problem and I can begin to feel better.

Focusing on the causes of our problems can make us feel worse than our actual problems.

When it comes to your own mental health and well-being, however, sometimes not knowing why is the best thing for you. Sometimes obsessing about, overanalyzing, and trying to unravel the mysteries in your life is exactly why you're feeling so shitty to begin with. When you shift away from asking *why* all the time and begin to accept that certain things are the way they are just because, you'll be amazed at how quickly that stick will begin to come out of your ass and how much better you'll begin to feel.

Many years ago, when I first began experiencing horrible anxiety and panic attacks all the time, I was determined to get to the bottom of it and figure out why. I examined every part of my life in great detail and ended up driving myself crazy over it. The harder I tried to understand it, the worse I felt. *Was it my personality? Was it my reactions to life events? Was it because I was so uptight and had a stick up my ass all the time? Was it because I had a chemical imbalance in my brain? Was it my upbringing? Was it hereditary?*

Why does it matter?

I'm not sure what happened, but one day I had this "ah-ha" moment where it hit me: *Why does it matter?* I can't even begin to tell you the weight that was lifted. It felt great. My attitude all of a sudden changed to: *Maybe it is something hereditary. Maybe it is my personality. Maybe it is because I always have a stick up my ass. Maybe it is a chemical imbalance. Maybe I'm just an anxious person. Maybe it's a lot of these things.* It didn't matter. Trying to figure it out was doing me no good. What helped was focusing on my recovery and getting better.

Now I apply this same method to so many different things in my own life, and so should you. What are you spending too much time trying to figure out that's sucking the life right out of you? Stop always trying to determine why you do the things you do. Stop trying to figure out what's wrong with you. Stop asking a million questions about why you can't find a life partner who makes you happy. Stop driving yourself up a wall trying to learn why you're able to lose 10 pounds only to put it right back on. Stop trying to figure out why your cholesterol is high and just focus on getting it down. Stop trying to figure out why you suck at golf and just enjoy it. Stop trying to figure out why you are an introvert and learn to accept it and even use it to your advantage. Stop trying to figure out why you like things that other people don't. Just pull the stick out of your ass, stop asking why, and begin to accept that certain things are the way they are just because—and that's okay. Then put your energy into focusing on the solution.

HELL YEAH!— PROFANITIES HELP

> When shit brings you down, just say "F*ck it," and eat yourself some motherf*cking candy.
> —David Sedaris

I have a confession: I love to curse! If you don't like that, well, too damn bad.

We're taught early on that cursing is vulgar, unacceptable behavior and something we shouldn't do. Maybe you got in trouble as a kid for saying a swear word in school. Maybe during an outing with friends, you used some words that offended people sitting at the next table over. Perhaps at some point in your life, someone told you to watch your language. There are indeed times and places you really do need to be careful with the words you use.

Don't run your potty mouth in professional and other inappropriate settings.

In fact, I'm not encouraging you to run your potty mouth at work or in other professional settings. I'm not telling you to use profanities around your in-laws or other important people in your life. I'm definitely not recommending you encourage your kids to curse, either. In fact, quite the opposite around the kiddos. Cursing is also probably a bad idea on a first date because honestly, cursing isn't sexy.

The swear jar—your secret to saving money...and relieving stress.

Cursing isn't sophisticated. Cursing isn't attractive. Cursing doesn't show good manners. Cursing won't impress anyone. However, there are many benefits to cursing, in my experience. I've found personally that:

- it relieves stress and tension,
- it can increase pain tolerance,
- people who curse are sometimes smarter than people who don't,
- it highlights our emotional response to something,
- it is a temporary release from normal social constraints,
- it shows self-confidence,

- it might mean you're more honest,
- there are mental and physical health benefits,
- and my personal favorite: it just feels GOOD.

It's actually quite funny because around most people, I hardly ever use swear words. Unless someone is a close friend and I feel really comfortable around them, I'm careful with what I say. I'll watch how they use their words first rather than just assuming it's okay to curse. Even around people I'm really close with, I still tend to hold back the F-bombs and other potentially offensive words. I hardly even ever curse around my wife.

My internal dialogue is filled with expletives.

When I'm talking to myself, however—something that I do all the time—every other word is an expletive. I pull that cursing stick right out of my ass, and off to town I go. I don't regret that. I don't feel bad about it. I like that about me. It feels good, and for me, it's a healthy coping mechanism. It's how I handle stress and all the negative shit that I can't control. Swear words are constantly going through my mind, and when I'm alone I like to say them as loudly and boldly as possible.

The other thing I like about cursing is that it really emphasizes what you are saying or feeling. I was in the grocery store the other day, and they didn't have the waffles I like to eat. Sure, I could have said, "Why are they out of my waffles?" But it really made the point and made me feel good to instead say, "Damn it. They don't have the motherf*cking waffles again." One time I was trying to hang a picture. I was barefoot. I accidentally dropped the hammer on my foot. I suppose I could have said, "Ouch! That really hurts." But it really made me feel better to scream, "Oh shit! My toe!"

When it comes to cursing, I don't think you should feel bad about doing it. Don't beat yourself up over it. If someone doesn't like that about you, it's their problem, not yours.

SOME TIPS TO FLIP

> It always seems impossible until it's done.
> —Nelson Mandela

I'm not one for motivational bullshit. Generally speaking, I believe it's short-lived and oftentimes misleading advice coming from people who don't know what they're talking about. I would always sit in the school assemblies listening to the guest motivational speakers they would bring in, and I would think, *This guy is full of shit.* You'll never hear me say things like, "You can do anything you set your mind to," or "All of your dreams and desires can come true." If that kind of stuff does it for you, then that's great. It's just not my thing.

However, with that said, I do like to engage in what I call *flipping shit on its ass.* Maybe that is the same thing that the motivational speakers call "doing the impossible," but I think it's more fun to say "flipping shit on its ass."

Flipping shit on its ass is taking back control.

What exactly does it mean to "flip shit on its ass"? It might sound like it's turning a bad scenario on its head, but for me, it means a couple of things. Mostly, it's taking a strong position and standing up for what you believe in, even when people disagree with you. It's staring down the face of adversity, putting the cart before the horse, because deep down you just know what you're doing will work. It's being your own person and not going down the same path everyone else takes. It's bouncing back from a terrible setback and taking control of shit that's been standing in your way for a very long time.

Flipping that shit on its ass is also very important when it comes to your recovery from a mental health condition. I had so many days I was out there trying to do this or that when the physical symptoms from the panic attacks got to be too much. It would have been so easy to give up and just go home (and sometimes I did), but I would try to push a little more, drive a little farther out of my comfort zone, go up a few more floors in that really tall building, approach a total stranger and initiate a conversation, ride the elevator by myself, or work through the terrible symptoms and try to calm down instead of running.

This approach can be applied to any situation in your life. There's this company in my industry that I've followed for quite some time, and I would possibly consider working for them. I could have gone through the usual channels, filled out an application online, waited for a position to open up, maybe get a call somewhere down the road, and more than likely have it go nowhere. Instead, I found the CEO's contact information and told her we have to meet. She agreed, and we are having coffee very soon.

What if you've got extreme agoraphobia and can't leave the house? Take a few steps onto your front porch. Stop and bring your anxiety down. Do it 10 more times until you get comfortable. Then take a few more steps away from the porch.

What if you have a really difficult decision to make and you can't make up your mind? Follow your gut instinct and take action today.

What if you keep struggling to lose weight or make money? Take the steps you need to take to start moving closer to the end goal.

Learning how to flip that shit on its ass is one of the best tools you can add to your emotional health arsenal. I know I'm making it sound easy. I know things are not always so simple. I know life doesn't always play out like we want. I know how debilitating it can be to work through a mental illness. I also know that no matter how bad it is, sometimes you just have to say, "Enough," pull the stick out of your ass, and move in the direction you want to go despite your fears.

WHEN YOU DON'T KNOW WHAT TO DO, JUST GET STARTED

> The secret of getting ahead is getting started.
> —Mark Twain

Have you ever felt incredibly overwhelmed and didn't know where to begin? It's an everyday occurrence for me. I wake up, look at the mountain of clutter on my desk, see all the e-mails that piled up overnight, look at what activities the kids have after school, look at the long list of things my wife wants me to do, and I'm done. I'm ready to go back to bed.

Even when I finally settle down for the morning and get going on my work, sometimes I don't even know what to do first. I'll have five deadlines coming up, ten different articles to write, six phone calls to return, and more. I'm not very good at planning things out, and I prefer to do things when I'm in the mood to do them, so I just jump in and get started where it feels right. That's been the secret for me in anything I have ever done.

Focus on the freedom that comes when your to-do list is done.

It was a Sunday morning, and my wife had taken the kids out for the day with some friends. I was looking forward to having a day all by myself. Unfortunately, she had other plans, and left me this long-ass list of stuff to do—from grocery shopping and laundry to cleaning the house and making dinner. So much for my fun day alone! "Where the hell do I even begin?" I said to myself. I spent 10 minutes just staring at the list until I realized I was wasting time. The quicker I burned through her list, the more time I would have to myself. And with that, I just jumped in, throwing the clothes in the washer while picking up the house, then putting the clothes in the dryer and heading out to the store. I got home, put the groceries away, and then put the laundry away. I bought a slow cooker dinner at the store because that would just sit there for a few hours without me having to do anything. A few hours later, everything was practically done, and the rest of the day was mine. Of course, I was kind of tired by then, but that's okay.

The point is, I was inundated with a lot of shit. After stalling long enough, I finally pulled the stick out of my ass and just jumped in. I didn't give it any thought. I just jumped in and started doing things. One by one, my to-do list got smaller until it was done.

I see this all the time with people. My kids, for example, will come home and think about all the homework they have to do. "What should I do first?" my daughter will ask. I'll tell her, "Just start. Start with whatever you feel like doing first, but the quicker you get it all done the more time you have to play."

Don't think! Do.

Just get started. Don't think about how to do it. Don't think about how overwhelming it is. Just get moving. Start crossing shit off your list, and you'll start to pick up momentum and burn through it before you know it.

Will this strategy work for everyone and everything? Of course not. If you're the super analytical type who needs to see the entire plan and all the minute details, then this might not be for you. But otherwise, just jump in and get started. That's the key to getting things done, whether it's schoolwork, job-related work, errands, chores, or anything else. Just get started, and the rest will follow.

Part 2
PROTECTING YOUR MENTAL HEALTH

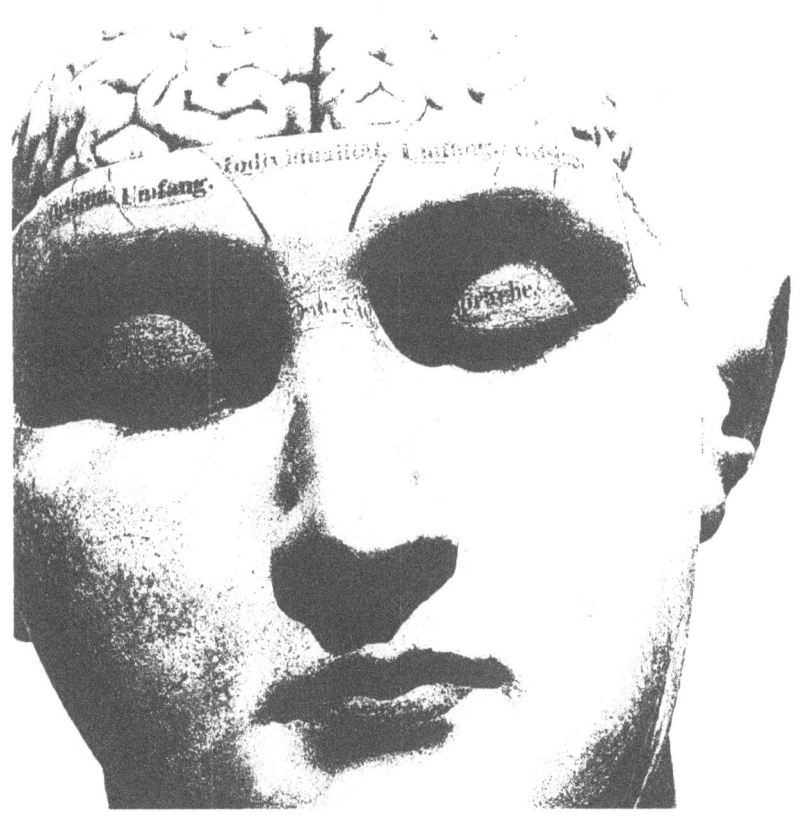

EMOTIONAL PAIN IS THE BIGGEST AND MOST DANGEROUS STICK IN THE ASS

> But pain's like water. It finds a way to push through any seal. There's no way to stop it. Sometimes you have to let yourself sink inside of it before you can learn how to swim to the surface.
>
> —Katie Kacvinsky

When we talk about the journey of pulling the stick out of your ass, some topics are a bit lighthearted, while others take a more serious tone. This is, in fact, one of those more serious topics and may very well be one of the most important ones in this book. Emotional pain is something we all deal with at one time or another and in different ways, and it must be handled quickly and properly.

Oftentimes the outside appearance conceals inner turmoil.

Robin Williams. Kate Spade. Anthony Bourdain. All three committed suicide. Worst of all, nobody saw it coming. These celebrities had fortune, fame, and a seemingly perfect life. But really, deep down inside, they were suffering, and it hurt so much that they decided to end it all. Emotional pain is a silent killer because the sufferer can hide it so well that many times, nobody can ever tell. Everything looks great on the outside, but inside it's a very different story. That's why many times, the life of the party, the one who seems to be having the most fun of all is the person who is suffering the most.

Emotional pain is a bitch. Emotional pain is a major stick in the ass. Emotional pain does not discriminate against any particular age group, ethnicity, religion, or region. Everyone deals with emotional pain at one time or another. For some, it's temporary and occurs in response to certain events. For others, it is a real uphill battle against major depression. In either case, emotional pain must be addressed. This is no joke and has caused way too many people to kill themselves.

Emotional pain can manifest as sadness, anger, jealousy, hurt, a disconnect, a lack of interest in things, guilt, not loving who you are, not believing in yourself, feeling like a failure, stress, and really, mental anguish of any kind. Emotional pain doesn't just feel bad; it affects your body too. Emotional pain will turn into physical pain and problems—for example, stomachaches, high blood pressure, heart palpitations, headaches, cramps, muscle tightness, fatigue, and more.

Sometimes it's difficult to identify the cause of emotional pain.

Sometimes you are keenly aware of the cause of your pain. It could be that you had a falling out with someone close to you. Maybe a close friend moved far away. Perhaps you lost your job or are going through a breakup. Maybe your dog recently passed away. Other times, however, you are not aware of the cause of your pain. Yes, it's true—you can have episodes of sadness, anger, self-doubt, and so many other emotions and have no idea why. Ever wake up and just feel off? Ever sit there thinking, *What the hell is wrong with me? Why do I feel so shitty? Why am I so drained?* That's emotional pain standing in the way.

It doesn't matter how you resolve emotional pain, just that you work to address it. Here are a few ways to do just that:

- **Talk to someone—anyone.** I don't care who you talk to; just talk to someone. We all tend to hold things in, but when you are hurting emotionally, this is the time to get it out. It can be a close friend whom you trust, a family member, therapist, or anyone. Just talk about your feelings with someone.

- **Journal about it.** I'm going to be honest with you. Until I sat down to write this book, I thought journaling was stupid and pointless. Boy was I wrong. If you can't talk it out with someone, write about it. You have to get it off your chest, and writing or typing about it feels so good. It's a great release. Writing this book has completely changed my perspective on how much better writing about something can make you feel.
- **Address the real problem behind the pain.** If you can identify the reason for your emotional pain, fix it. If it's someone in your life or you're in a bad relationship, work it out with them or get away from them. If it's pressure at work, ask a co-worker for help or address it with your boss. If you don't like how you look, make a commitment to lose weight by eating better and getting more exercise. Whatever it is, you have to address it or it won't get better.
- **Don't let it fester.** The more you ignore it and just let it sit there, the more powerful the pain will get and the more you will hurt. The sooner you can address it, the better. Emotional pain

that goes unresolved for years leads to so many mental and physical health problems.
- **Get off your ass.** When you're suffering from emotional pain it can be easy to become a deer in headlights and just freeze up because of all that is taking place around you and how awful you feel. Try to get moving, even just a little bit, every day. Go outside. Go for a walk. Go for a drive. Meet someone you like for a small amount of time. Just do something. Staying still or shutting yourself up in the house and letting the pain absorb you is only going to make it worse.
- **Learn coping skills.** Coping skills are essential for handling emotional pain. Find the tools that work best for you and your particular pain. It can be absolutely any healthy coping mechanism that helps relieve your pain. Drugs and alcohol might seem like good choices in the interim, but they usually provide a temporary reprieve in the short term and intensify the pain in the long run. Seek healthier options.
- **Be realistic and honest about depression.** Sometimes it's easy to find the root cause of emotional pain. Other times, it's not. If you can't figure it out, or if you are trying to fix things and you're not feeling better, be honest with yourself and recognize that you need to get professional help. We all suffer with emotional pain at times,

but when things don't get better, you might be dealing with clinical depression.[2]

---

[2] This chapter is not intended to be taken as medical advice and should not serve as a substitute for screening and diagnosis from a medical doctor. Talk to a trained medical professional to be screened for depression.

MENTAL ILLNESS IS NOT A DEATH SENTENCE

> I wish people could understand that the brain is the most important organ in our body. Just because you can't see mental illness like you could see a broken bone doesn't mean it's not as detrimental or devastating to a family or individual.
>
> —Demi Lovato

I want to get serious in this chapter. There will be no talking about sticks in the ass here. This is by far the most important chapter in this book.

It's time to end the stigma surrounding mental illness.

If you suffer from any type of mental illness, I applaud you. I have immense respect for you. I'm sorry for your pain and suffering. I'm sorry for how many people in the world today might stigmatize you. I've never really understood what's so hard to accept and understand about mental health conditions. They are no different than any other health condition. According to society, it's perfectly acceptable to seek medical care if you have a heart condition, cancer, or any type of physical health ailment—but if you're suffering from depression, anxiety, bipolar disorder, or another psychiatric illness, it's time to put up the red flags because too many people still deem it as abnormal. It's unbelievable—and 100 percent unacceptable—considering everything we know about the brain, that in today's world you might still be labeled as "different" or "strange" for having a mental illness. This is wrong. You are neither of these things. You are capable. You are worthy, and you are not alone. You are deserving of a joy-filled life, surrounded by loving and supportive individuals.

Many years ago, when I was in my early 20s, I was in the midst of my battle with panic disorder. Those closest to me were very supportive about it. Even with their encouragement, I was always apprehensive about telling people, even though it would have made my life easier in many ways and taken the pressure off trying to hide it. I was so scared that they would look at me differently, and I didn't want that.

We can't control everything that goes on in our body.

I also worried that my panic attacks were a sign of weakness or some other fault that I should have been able to prevent. Maybe there were some things about my personality and behavior I could have changed sooner that would have made a difference. The truth is, it wasn't my fault. It's the same reason why some people eat super healthy diets and exercise every day but are still walking around with heart disease. We can control a lot of what happens in our body, but we can't control it all. Sometimes things just happen. The brain is pretty complex, and chemical makeup and imbalances play a big role in all of this.

Through my recovery, my views have changed quite dramatically. I still deal with the phobic thoughts and personality, and the panic will rear its ugly face every once in a while. I generally don't just volunteer this information, but I'm not afraid to talk about it or admit that I struggled (and sometimes still do). The funniest thing happens when you do share it: people respond by saying something along the lines of, "I too suffered from...," or, "My sister also has..." That's because mental health problems are more common than we realize. In fact, whatever the statistics look like, I'm willing to bet the numbers are much greater simply because most people won't disclose their mental health struggles.

Mental Illness Is Not a Death Sentence

You are not alone.

I want you to know that if you are struggling with a mental illness or even suspect that you have one, please know that you are not alone. There are plenty of people who have been in your shoes and can relate. I was thickheaded and convinced that I would never recover from panic disorder. I had days when I could barely get out the front door or even drive down the street. I passed up job offers because they were too far away, high up in a building, or required a lot of travel. I lost some friends because I couldn't go out, couldn't be a passenger in their car, couldn't eat comfortably in a restaurant with them and just have fun. Am I cured? No, but I am recovered. I can tell you it's a million times better on this side of the picture. Believe me: if I can do it, so can you. No matter what condition you are struggling with, please get help. Talk to someone. Find a doctor who gets it. Talk to a friend or family member. Find a support group. Just do something. Doing nothing only makes it harder.

Please don't ever consider suicide. There's no going back. If you or someone you know is feeling suicidal, please get help immediately or call the National Suicide Prevention Hotline at 1-800-273-8255.

I truly believe that if more people sought treatment for their mental health challenges, the world would be a better place. You know what else I really believe? If everyone, even people without a true mental health condition, sought counseling or simply a way to sort out their thoughts and emotions, we'd all be better off. There'd be less fighting and hatred, more love and compassion, and more living in harmony. While we can't wait for the world to change its ways, we can each take the necessary steps to care for our own health and well-being. I hope you will be proactive in your own treatment and recovery, as well as supportive of those around you who may be struggling.[3]

---

[3] This chapter is not intended to be taken as medical advice. Seek the help of a trained medical professional for an individualized treatment and recovery plan. If you are struggling with suicidal thoughts, please call 911 or the National Suicide Prevention Hotline at 1-800-273-8255 immediately.

HOLY HYPOCHONDRIAC

> After obsessively googling symptoms for four hours, I discovered "obsessively googling symptoms" is a symptom of hypochondria.
> —Stephen Colbert

I was 20 years old and sitting in the waiting room at the cardiology office. Everyone else was three or four times my age. The nurse opened the door and called my name. I stood up, and all the elderly people in the room just stared at me. The nurse said, "Where's your dad? It's time for his test." I said, "No, it's me. I'm the patient," to which she responded, "Oh, sorry, we just don't see many people your age around here." It got worse. The ultrasound tech walked into the room and said, "Hey, I remember you from a few years ago." It was embarrassing, but when you're convinced something is wrong and you're a hypochondriac, you'll go to great extremes to prove yourself right.

I've suffered from every disease known to man.

I was a big hypochondriac when I was younger. In fact, it's amazing I'm still around today, because by now I think I suffered from every possible horrible disease known to man. Heck, I think I even had some that were never discovered before. Pain anywhere near my chest or down my arm? You got it—heart attack. Headache? Brain tumor. Stomachache? Appendicitis. There was one night I couldn't remember a few things and I swore I was going crazy and losing my mind. I worked myself into a huge panic attack and landed in the ER.

Being a hypochondriac is like having a huge stick in your ass all the time. Every little pain in your body or the feeling of being off just ever so slightly turns into the biggest ordeal. *Oh my God, this is it. What if I'm having a heart attack? What if it's cancer? What if I just drop dead right here and now? I think I should go get some tests run to be sure.* Oh man. It sucks!

Most of the time, the worry is unjustified—and damaging to your health.

In time, as I recovered from anxiety and panic attacks, I started to pull that stick out of my ass and ease up about every little ache and pain. Yes, sometimes there is a reason you are feeling something. However, much of the time, it's nothing at all.

Think of it this way: the human body is a very complex machine made up of roughly 37.2 trillion cells, 206 bones, more than enough blood to fill a one-gallon container of milk, a muscular system, digestive system, respiratory system, urinary system, reproductive system, endocrine system, circulatory system, lymphatic system, nervous system, sensory organs, and integumentary system. All of this has to work in harmony so that we can function and stay healthy. Just as you sometimes hear an unexplained noise in your home or car, you're going to feel things in your body that may seem strange or draw your attention. Sometimes you need to investigate further, but much of the time it's nothing more than just a normal little feeling, no matter how weird it seems.

Here are some stick-pulling tips I've incorporated into my own life that will help you stop being a hypochondriac and reduce your health anxiety:

- **Get a check-up.** This is geared especially toward men, many of whom are notorious for avoiding the doctor at all costs. You need to pull the stick out of your ass and go for a yearly physical. If you are seeing a specialist for a specific condition, keep those regular doctor appointments and take your medications as prescribed. Taking control of your health reduces health anxiety.

- **Be cautious, but don't overreact.** People get sick. People experience pain and discomfort. This is normal, especially with aging. Always lean on the side of caution, and if something doesn't seem right get it checked out.
- **Make healthier choices.** This means eating healthier, exercising more, and reducing stress. It's hard to be perfect or 100 percent compliant, so give yourself a break from time to time. But leading a better overall lifestyle improves your mental and physical health and reduces your chance of illness.
- **Educate yourself about any health conditions you do have.** If you have been diagnosed with any mental or physical health condition, learn the facts about your illness. Know what to expect, what is normal, and what is not normal. It can also help to find a support group of other people who are dealing with the same condition. Eliminating surprises minimizes health anxiety.
- **Dr. Google is your friend and foe.** The Internet can be a great tool to find information quickly; however, it can also be a really bad thing for a hypochondriac. If you're not experiencing symptoms of an illness but then read that some people are, it's amazing how quickly you can start feeling those same exact things too. Be careful what you read online.

- **Get help.** Health anxiety is a real problem for many people. If you're struggling with it, reach out to a mental health professional, because there are many great therapies and medications that can help.[4]

---

[4] This chapter is not intended to be taken as medical advice. To be screened for hypochondria and other anxiety disorders and/or to seek treatment for them, please consult a trained medical professional.

SPREAD YOUR WINGS AND FLY

> Once you have tasted flight, you will forever walk the earth with your eyes turned skyward, for there you have been, and there you will always long to return.
> —Leonardo da Vinci

No, this is not a cliché chapter about releasing your inhibitions and soaring into the sky to attain "massive success" in life. This is a chapter about flying...literally.

As you've probably recognized by now, flying on airplanes is a very meaningful and important topic for me, not only because a lot of people struggle with it, but also because it's something I love to do. However, despite my passion for airplanes, for the longest time I was unable to fly without severe anxiety. If you don't have any trouble with flying and this is not a big stick in your ass, you might not care to read this chapter. However, if you have difficulty getting on airplanes, whether you are extremely terrified and can't do it at all or just get a little nervous, I believe it will help you tremendously.

Airplanes and panic attacks are unpleasant bedfellows.

I'm writing this chapter on a flight from Atlanta to Las Vegas, where I'm giving a speech tomorrow. The total flight time is four hours and five minutes. That's significant because not long ago, a flight of that duration would have been out of the question for me. *Four hours on an airplane? Are you effing kidding me?* I never would have thought it would be possible for me to handle it, but now I could sit here all day. It's my happy place. In fact, I'm addicted. Yes, I have a flying addiction.

I've been fascinated by planes since I was a kid. I loved going to the airport and watching them take off and land. My grandfather would travel for business, and I always enjoyed listening to his stories about his flight adventures. Oh, if he could only see how far the airplanes of today have come. He gave me my first book about airplanes, which detailed how they progressed from the Wright Brothers' model to more advanced versions over the years. I was hooked instantly. Isn't it ironic, don't you think, that someone could have such a fascination with something and at the same time be totally terrified of it? Let me clarify: it wasn't the airplanes or the flying that scared me. It was the anxious feelings that came as a result of flying that I had the hardest time dealing with.

The problem is airplanes and panic attacks don't go well together. And believe me, I've had my share of them on airplanes. There are so many triggers for anxiety and panic attacks on airplanes: a confined space (which seems to get more crammed by the day as airlines add more seats and decrease legroom), heights, lack of control over the aircraft, turbulence, and just having nowhere to run and escape to.

Practice might not make perfect, but it can make you more comfortable.

The first time I flew when panic attacks became a real problem for me was in 1999. It was a quick flight from Fort Lauderdale to Tampa, roughly 40 minutes of actual flight time. I never prepared so much for something in my life. I made trips to the airport every day just watching the planes come and go. At that time, anyone could get past security, and I would sit in the terminal for hours and watch the people get on and off the planes. Just being there every day helped desensitize me. Did it make it easy when it came time to do it? Heck no! But the airport felt familiar, and familiar is your friend when you have severe anxiety and panic attacks.

I anticipated that flight for weeks, and several times was literally sick to my stomach thinking about it.

The days leading up to my flight, I went to the airport and watched the same exact flight I would be taking depart. I watched the boarding process. I wanted to know everything that happened so there were no surprises. The other thing that helped, besides wanting to fly again, was that my girlfriend was living in Tampa at the time. So, there was definitely motivation for me to travel because I could get to spend a few days with her.

I did this trip several times. Eventually, I was able to fly farther distances. Before I knew it, I was able to go from Florida to the Northeast, with a stopover in Atlanta. At the time, two shorter flights were more manageable for me. Other people wouldn't like that and would probably prefer having one longer flight. These days, I do, too. Whatever you have to do to make it easier for yourself is what you do, at least in the beginning.

I would fly every so often, but I never became fully comfortable with the process. It was even iffy whether I would be able to fly from Miami to Jamaica for our honeymoon, but I pulled it off. I didn't really get good at flying until I started doing it regularly. I started my own business in 2010, and for the last 10 years I've been doing about 20 trips a year. Flying over and over again has made me comfortable with it. Am I perfect? No, I have my moments. But I bet I'm more comfortable than most people on the plane. Rarely does turbulence bother me unless it's really bad. I've had my share of flight delays, being stranded on the tarmac for hours, diversions, aborted takeoffs, missed approaches, go-arounds—you name it.

You *can* overcome your fear of flying.

I believe that flying is one of the more challenging phobias to overcome, but if you love it as much as I do (or don't love it but just need to do it) and put in the work, it is doable. Not only is it doable—it's possible to be comfortable and perhaps even learn to enjoy it. Ironically enough, even with all the flying I do today, I still fly that FLL-TPA route where it all started several times a year, and I never take my ability to do so for granted. Below are some tips and tricks for overcoming a fear of flying.

- **Familiarize yourself with statistics.** Reassure yourself by researching the statistics on flying and how safe it really is. You're way more likely to be killed or injured driving to the grocery store than on an airplane.
- **Start with a shorter flight.** Some people suggest taking a longer flight your first time to give yourself a chance to calm down and watch the fear come and go. I'm not a fan of this approach because I think it's going to be too overwhelming. Make it easy on yourself and start small. Also, if you give yourself a short distance to start with, you take the pressure off in knowing that if it really is that bad, you can always drive back. That might sound like an "out," and it is. Remember,

in the beginning, do whatever you have to and make it easy on yourself.
- **Visit the airport and soak it all in.** Granted, this was easy for me because it was something I liked to do. Whether you like the idea of it or not, just get there. Figure out where things are. Know where you'll have to go when your day comes. Get comfortable being there. Sit on a bench and watch the people come and go. Park near the runway or in a viewing area and watch the planes. When it becomes boring and your anxiety levels stay low, you're ready for the next step.
- **Watch some videos on YouTube.** You can see the cabin of just about any aircraft from any airline. Remember, the idea is to get comfortable and know what things look like ahead of time. Eliminate the surprises.
- **Know what flight you'll be taking at least a few weeks ahead of time.** Track the flight in the days leading up to your trip. While you can't predict weather or mechanical delays, you can see if there tends to be any patterns with the schedule. You're also reinforcing the fact that this same exact flight operates successfully every single day.
- **Bring tools (distractions) with you to pass the time and take your mind off your symptoms.** Maybe it's some games like a word search or crossword puzzle. It could be games on your

smartphone. Bring a book—something humorous and light-hearted or perhaps a consuming thriller, whichever will best distract you and make you feel comfortable.
- **Eat Warheads or another extremely sour candy.** Pop one as you take the runway and the pilot increases thrust. You won't have time to be anxious because you'll be so overwhelmed by the intense taste in your mouth.
- **Find or create a mental activity in your surroundings.** I don't bring much these days when I fly, so if I start to feel my anxiety levels rising, I pick up the in-flight magazine and start circling every letter R that I can find. Many airplanes are equipped with in-flight entertainment systems, so if you're on a plane like that you might get into a TV show or a game that occupies your mind.
- **Watch your anxiety levels go up and down and go with it.** Remember, even when they get really high, it might be uncomfortable and scary, but nothing bad will happen.
- **When you get a case of the "oh shits" and you realize where you are and what you're doing, just stop.** Slow your breathing. Slow your body. Get distracted.
- **Pick a seat that makes you comfortable.** When I was getting back into flying, I always had to sit near the back of the plane and in an aisle seat. This made me feel better to think if I freaked out,

fewer people could see. It also made the plane feel larger, and I didn't feel as closed in seeing everything in front of me. I still like to be near the back, but I can sit wherever these days. I'm even comfortable with the window seat and love to look out.

- **Don't let a bad experience stop you from trying again.** Even after I've done this what seems like a million times now, one day not long ago I had a horrific panic attack while on that very short flight from Fort Lauderdale to Tampa. Bad experiences happen for a lot of different reasons, even when you get good and comfortable with something. In this particular instance, I got lax, wasn't prepared, and had just gotten off a plane a few days earlier and thought this was going to be easy. When you get cocky like that, it's going to come back and bite you in the ass. Try and learn from your bad experiences, but don't let them stop you.
- **If you have a tough time with flying (or any other phobia) remember the acronym HALTS**: hungry, angry, lonely, tired, or stressed. If any one of these things is going on, you're going to be more susceptible to anxiety. It's a great lesson I learned from a mentor many years ago.[5]

---

5   This chapter is not intended to be taken as medical advice. If you struggle with anxiety or panic disorder, work with your own medical doctor to create an individualized treatment plan.

I HAVE SOMETHING TO SAY BUT I'M SOCIAL PHOBIC

> Be who you are and say what you feel, because those who mind don't matter and those who matter don't mind.
>
> —Dr. Seuss

I just attended a wedding for a family friend. It was a beautiful affair at an excellent facility with lots of music, dancing, and conversation among friends, family, and neighbors. It was a very joyous occasion. For me, however, it was a total nightmare. It was exhausting. It was painful. It was embarrassing, although nobody else probably noticed my awkwardness. It wasn't just this particular social gathering—most events like this would be enough to make me feel this way.

Social phobia can be situational.

This may sound surprising coming from someone who works in the media and even does public speaking. The thing with social phobia is that it can be situational, and for me it's less of an issue inside a professional setting and more of a problem in those casual social situations.

Social settings are really difficult for people with social phobia. There's no other way to say it other than it sucks big time. You feel miserable, depressed, and removed from the party, just sitting there on your own, trying to make the time go by. Although I am someone who emphasizes the importance of removing the stick from one's ass, I looked like I had a really big stick up my ass at that party. The truth is, I did, and this was not one that was going to come out easily, if at all. Social situations are one of the few occasions where the almighty stick still gets the best of me.

Social phobia isn't about wanting to be alone; it's about wanting to feel included.

What people don't get is you genuinely want to have a good time and be part of the conversation, but it's hard—really, really hard. I had such a stomachache when I got home—not just from the nerves, but from all the food I kept stuffing in my mouth so I wouldn't have to talk to anyone. At least it was good food, for the most part.

Let me share with you a few of the thousands of negative, self-destructive thoughts that consumed me that evening:

- I have nothing interesting to say.
- People don't want to talk to me.
- I'm so boring.
- I'm embarrassing my wife.
- Nobody likes me.
- I look foolish.
- Man, I'm making an ass of myself.
- Look at all those people dancing and having fun. Everyone would laugh at me if I got up there.
- I think people are looking at me.
- I think they are talking about me and making fun of me.
- I wonder what the hosts think of me right now.
- What if the DJ calls me out?

Can you see why I was so tired and defeated by the end of the night? I never even gave myself a chance. I self-destructed before the party even started.

In this chapter, I'd like to bring some awareness to an anxiety disorder with which so many people silently suffer. Like many other mental health issues, it's not one that gets a lot of attention, mostly because people are afraid of how they will be perceived by others. I don't have all the answers on how to cope with any mental illness, but with this one I have fewer than others. I've been fortunate enough to get over a lot of my anxiety issues, but I still regularly battle social phobia. Sometimes I do manage to get through a social situation fairly unharmed, but many times it's a fight, if not utter torture, and I definitely come across like I have a big stick in my ass.

Even though I'm still working through my social phobia, there are a couple strategies I've found that are helpful for managing it:

- **Prep beforehand.** If you're attending the event with another person, discuss your social phobia with them ahead of time and come up with some talking points. Even if you're going solo, if you think of some go-to discussion topics ahead of time, you'll feel more comfortable joining in conversations. You'll also be better able to keep the dialogue within your comfort zone.
- **Speak with confidence even if it feels awkward**. You are probably feeling anything but comfortable and confident in the social situation, and as a result you may come across as soft-spoken. Do your best to make your voice heard. Push through the fear and speak boldly, with passion, and be sure to smile. Keep eye contact with the people with whom you are speaking. This shows confidence and will also make you feel more confident.

- **Have an exit plan.** Come up with some excuses for why you might have to leave early ahead of time. Not only that—but know where the actual exits are in the place where you're going. That way, if shit gets weird, awkward, or uncomfortable, or anything else goes awry, you know how and where to get the hell out. Having an exit plan is a helpful tool for people with social phobia and panic disorder, and sadly, it's also just great life advice these days.

If you're at a gathering with someone who struggles with social anxiety, there are things you can do to make it easier on them, to take the pressure off and make them feel more included. Trust me: even a little compassion, understanding, and support goes a long way.

To best support people with social anxiety...

- **Let them define their own boundaries.** Sometimes people with social phobia want to be alone. Sometimes they want to tag along because you are their safe person. Give them the space they need to be comfortable, whatever that looks like for them.
- **Do try and include them.** People with social phobia have a voice. They just have a difficult time getting the words out. Ask them questions.

Ask for their opinion. Ask them to recount that funny story you remember them telling. Don't constantly ask them questions, but if they are getting quiet then they probably are feeling anxious, so try to be inclusive when possible.
- **Don't try to figure them out.** You may not understand what people with social phobia are feeling or going through in the moment. In fact, you may never understand it. Just accept that and don't try to figure it all out.
- **Never ask, "Why are you being so quiet?"** The worst thing you can do is bring attention to the fact that social phobic people are keeping to themselves. They're struggling enough, and this is going to make them feel even more self-conscious and believe that everyone else is noticing and thinks differently of them. People with social phobia don't like their quietness to become the center of attention.
- **Don't belittle their attempts.** People with social anxiety may sometimes bring a bit of awkwardness with their attempts at speaking conversationally, but don't call it out. Just go along with it and smile. Asking something like, "What the heck was that?" is going to make them feel even worse and more self-conscious.
- **Be patient.** Anxiety comes in waves. Picture an ocean wave with highs and lows. One moment the anxiety can be so bad that sufferers are left

practically speechless and paralyzed. Other times it's not so bad, and they can voice their thoughts clearly. There will be times when they are doing really well and then all of a sudden lose some of the ground they had gained. Be patient with your friends or loved ones with social phobia.

- **Know when to push them and when to back off.** One of the great attributes of supporting people with social phobia or any anxiety disorder is simply understanding when they need a confidence boost and encouragement to give something a try. Sometimes, however, pushing is the worst thing you can do, and it's best to simply back off. In time, you will learn to figure out what works best, when they need your help, as well as when to back off altogether.[6]

---

[6] This chapter is not intended to be taken as medical advice. If you struggle with anxiety or panic disorder, work with a trained medical professional to create an individualized treatment plan.

TAKING MEDICATION DOESN'T MEAN YOU'RE WEAK

> There's no right or wrong way to manage your mental illness. You are not less of a person for needing medication or having to go to therapy multiple times a week. If something helps your mental health, take the time to do it. Don't stop, no matter what other people think.
>
> —Hayley Lyvers

We have a real problem in American society: people who have a stick up their ass and a problem with other people taking medication for their mental health. They see mental illness as this thing that people make up or use as a cop-out to get out of things they don't want to do. Unlike a cut or scrape, mental illness is not visible, so they think it must not be real. Although you can't see it, it is very, very real. In fact, we know that several factors come into play with mental health, and a chemical imbalance in the brain is one of those things. Medication can help restore the balance of these chemicals like serotonin, norepinephrine, and dopamine. Some people need medication for the short term. Others need it for life. Without it, some people can't even function.

Mental illness is not a cop-out.

When I was at my worst with panic attacks, I would carry around prescription anti-anxiety medication in my pocket. When things got bad, I would take one. It would help in those moments of extreme panic or when I was feeling tense or anxious. Unfortunately, this wasn't enough because I started having trouble functioning, and even going more than a few blocks from home became challenging. My doctor didn't want me continually turning to something that I could get addicted to, and he also suspected a chemical imbalance, so he suggested I start taking a prescription antidepressant, which is also commonly prescribed to treat severe anxiety and panic attacks. I was terrified of this.

For years, I fought taking medication. I was okay with over-the-counter medicine, but other things scared me. I didn't want to become addicted or rely on meds. One time, when I had a really bad sinus infection, I had a terrible reaction to the antibiotics I was given. This has made taking new medication more difficult for me because I'm always scared of how I'll react. In addition to fearing the health effects, at the time I believed that if I needed to take medication, I was weak and just covering up the problem. I was wrong.

After much back and forth, I ended up taking the antidepressant, and it helped me take control of my life. Does it eliminate anxiety, depression, or panic attacks altogether? Absolutely not. It reduces symptoms, makes them more manageable, and makes functioning possible. You still have to do the work, face your fears and phobias, and learn to work through the underlying issues, but medication certainly helps you get off your ass and get moving.

Consult your doctor about the potential benefits and drawbacks of taking any medication.

There are a lot of horror stories out there about different psychiatric medications. I can also tell you there are a lot of success stories like mine. When you reach the point that you want to try it or your doctor suggests it, don't be afraid to give it a go. The following are some general principles to keep in mind with regard to psychiatric drugs:

- **Medication is necessary for some people.** You wouldn't question taking medication for a heart condition or cancer, and you shouldn't hesitate

to take it for a mental health condition like anxiety, depression, or others if you need it.
- **If you need medication for your mental health and well-being, you are not weak.** You are not inferior to someone who doesn't need it. You are not any less of a person. Applaud yourself for taking control of your health.
- **Medication by itself may not be the solution to your problems.** It can play a big role in the process of taking back control of your life, but there may be underlying issues that need to be identified and treated with therapy.
- **If you are taking medication or thinking about taking it, find a psychiatrist you like and trust and follow his or her advice.** A lot of family physicians prescribe psychiatric medications, but I've always found that psychiatrists are much more knowledgeable in this area. It's a good idea to consult both if you're struggling with mental illness.[7]

---

[7] This chapter is not intended to be taken as medical advice. Always talk to your own medical doctor before starting, stopping, or changing medications.

FIND SAFETY AND COMFORT IN YOURSELF

> Having a safe space to imagine and dream and (re)invent yourself is the first step to being happy and successful, whatever road you choose to pursue.
> —Ashley Bryan

There's a place deep in the woods, sitting on a quiet lake, surrounded by really tall trees. The noise of the hustle and bustle of the city is long forgotten, and it's the most peaceful, relaxing place I've ever seen. Small waterfalls have formed, and you can hear a soothing sound as the water moves and falls among the different levels of rocks. There's a small house within walking distance with a fireplace and some comfortable couches on which you can sit or recline. There are no smartphones, computers, or other electronics. I'm not exactly sure where this place is, but in my mind I've been there thousands of times. The best part is, nobody has ever been there, and nobody can ever access it but me.

This is my place. This is where I go for a lot of different reasons, mostly when I need a break or to get away from something or someone. Many nights when I can't fall asleep, I close my eyes and come here just to sit and veg out, eventually falling asleep. Sometimes it's simply to relax. Other times it's to escape reality. Quite often, it's to let go of the stress and anxiety that has built up throughout the day.

Safe places don't have to be physical locations.

When I was recovering from panic disorder and learning to feel comfortable in public settings or when I was far from home, I was always looking for a safe place that was an external setting. Typically, it was a police station, fire station, hospital, or doctor's office. In my mind, these were signs of safety and security—places that could help me if I had a panic attack, lost control, and needed help calming down. It was awful because any time I had to go somewhere, I was pulling out the map and locating my safety spots for every second of the trip. I used to laugh at myself and think, "Imagine if I told anyone all that I had to do just to go out. What would they think if they knew I was always hoping an ambulance would be nearby?" As tough as it was, I was able to laugh about it, which was important. I knew I had to pull this stick out of my ass, even though it was a really tough one for me. Unfortunately, this is the hellish reality in which people with severe panic disorder live on a daily basis.

Even to this day, while I no longer rely on their proximity for comfort, it's still kind of a safe feeling when any of these places are nearby. However, these are all physical locations, and while in general there's nothing wrong with that, especially as you're beginning your recovery from an anxiety disorder, you want to get to a point where you do not depend on visiting a physical location to feel secure. I learned along my journey that I can be my own safe place. You can be your own safe place, too.

You can be your own safe place.

Whether it's the awful bodily symptoms of a panic attack, having to make a stressful decision, feeling overworked and overrun by your day-to-day tasks, or having trouble getting comfortable or relaxing, you have to be the one you rely on. In fact, not only is this a good habit to develop, but it's going to help you grow and become stronger in everything you do. When you really acknowledge that you are your own best friend, that safety resource you are looking for, and the one you can depend on, your inner confidence will skyrocket, because instead of always looking for and having to turn to outside forces, you'll be able to do anything.

This is often a hard concept for people with mental illness to really get comfortable with for a number of reasons, the most obvious being that most of us simply don't believe in ourselves and our own abilities. We believe we can't help ourselves, and so we rely on someone else to always be there for us. Asking for help, having a support person or someone to hold your hand, is perfectly acceptable at times. But the more you start to depend on *you*, the stronger you become, the more powerful you start to see yourself as, and eventually, you can help yourself feel better in any situation that life throws your way.

This doesn't mean you shut other people out or that you never have to turn to someone for help. I'm a big believer in asking people for help, as you've learned in an earlier chapter, but when it comes to feeling safe and reassured it's important to find security within yourself. When you are the one you run to, you are quickly on your way to overcoming your fears and worries, building your confidence, and truly being free.

Is it easy? Of course not. It is very doable, however. Start slow and begin looking inside yourself the next time you're not feeling right or you just need a break. The truth is, safety starts from within.

Here are some tips for creating your own safe space when anxiety becomes overpowering:

- **Identify a safe space location.** This can either be a physical location like a quiet bookstore or

neighborhood park to which you go or a place, like the house in the woods I described above, that you visualize in your head. This must be a place that you associate with comfort and safety—that makes you *feel safe* when you envision it or go to it. Think about what images or sensory perceptions you find comforting, and either find a physical location with those characteristics or create one in your mind.
- **Visit your safe space regularly to "check in."** To strengthen the positive associations you have with this place, take trips there—either in your thoughts or in reality—and spend time enjoying the sensations that arise from being in this safe space. Let the feel of this space—its temperature, sights, smells, etc.—etch itself on your brain. The more familiar it becomes to you, the easier it will be to return there mentally when you're not able to physically exit a triggering situation.
- **Shift your safe space into the realm of your thoughts.** If your safe space has been a physical location, replicate it within your mind so that it is internal rather than external to you. The goal is to stop relying on physically moving yourself to a specific location in order to cope with anxiety. If you can conjure the safe space within your mind, you can handle anxiety-inducing situations more easily and self-sufficiently.

- **Transfer these positive sensations to your self.** That's not a typo. I mean that you should take all the good, safety-inducing feelings you derive from your safe space and link them with your person, your psyche. If you can look inside and locate warmth, coziness, and other positive sensations within your being rather than within a real or imagined place, then you can gain the strength to handle anything life throws your way.[8]

---

8   This chapter is not intended to be taken as medical advice. If you struggle with anxiety or panic disorder, work with your own medical doctor to create an individualized treatment plan.

THIS IS HOW YOU TELL ANXIETY TO F*CK OFF

> The only way out is through.
> —Robert Frost

You never forget your first time. Oh wait, I wasn't talking about *that* first time.

Picture this: I'm sitting in the newsroom working. I have a phone in each ear. I'm holding the two-way radio in my left hand, communicating with the reporters and photographers in the field. I'm holding a pen in my right hand. Meanwhile, I have a producer shouting at me from the other side of the newsroom with a question. The police scanners are chirping full blast, and I hear that a little kid has just fallen into a pool, isn't breathing, and EMS is on the way. I need to get a crew there. Then, we miss an important satellite uplink to get some video to one of our affiliates across the country. Five other phones are ringing just waiting for me to answer them. It's 6:00 P.M. and the news is about to start, but I also need to watch the lead stories of our competitors to make sure they didn't one-up us on an important story. Holy shit, I'm losing it!

All of a sudden, something strange begins to happen to my body. I start to feel lightheaded and dizzy. My heart is pounding. My breathing becomes quick and shallow—I'm hyperventilating. I begin to shake. I feel like I'm going to pass out, but at the same time my mind is telling me to run because I'm about to die. The rest is a blur, but I took off and somehow got myself to the emergency room. They got an IV going, and before I knew it I was feeling pretty good. Make that really good! It was margarita time.

That's the quick description of a panic attack, and it was the very first one I ever experienced. For most people, anxiety is a normal part of life that comes and goes based on specific situations like public speaking or going to the dentist. For people with a true anxiety disorder, especially panic disorder, anything and everything can be a trigger. In fact, sometimes you can't even find the trigger; you just feel anxious. You could be sitting at home chilling in the living room and BAM, here come the horrible feelings.

But wait, there's more!

If that wasn't enough fun, it gets worse. Many people who suffer like I did become so terrified of having a panic attack in a public situation or a place where escape might not be so easy that they begin avoiding everything. They stop going out in public. They don't want to hang out with their friends. They don't travel. They can't get in a car unless they are driving and in control of the vehicle. Sometimes they are afraid to go anywhere alone and always need their "safe" person to accompany them. The circle of safety shrinks and shrinks until one day, they can't even leave their house. That's how debilitating this is. Even my description in these few paragraphs doesn't do justice to how awful this condition is.

I've come a long way in my recovery. I say "recovery" because I am recovered. I don't say "cured" because I'm not cured and I don't know that there is a cure. I can do most things with ease. Sometimes I still get a little anxiety. Once in a while, I still get those big, awful panic attacks. They usually don't last as long and aren't severe enough to send me to the ER, but they still knock me on my ass.

You have to expose yourself to the fear.

Facing anxiety and panic is one of the toughest things you will ever do. There are a lot of roads to recovery, things like medication and psychotherapy, but ultimately, to recover, you have to expose yourself to the fear. You have to say, "Screw it," enter the triggering situation, and walk right through that fear. It feels like jumping out of a plane and not knowing if you're wearing a parachute. When you learn to work through and de-escalate the uncomfortable physical sensations and flood of horrific thoughts going through your mind, no matter how scary they are, you are on your way to recovery.

The more you face it, the easier it becomes. With practice, it's possible to become comfortable in almost any situation. However, there may still be some situations that you never become completely comfortable with. A good example of this for me is heights. I can enjoy looking out from a tall building, but getting up there initially can be extremely difficult for me.

Your triggers can gain and lose power without your realizing it.

Finally, some situations might be easy to handle on some days and then out of nowhere, just when you think you've mastered them, they become almost impossible again. This happened to me recently. I was driving on the highway—something I don't have a problem with anymore—when out of nowhere I got kicked in the ass with a panic attack. The next time I had to get on the highway my mind wouldn't let me forget what happened. I had to fight with everything I had to get back on that particular stretch of road, and I did.

There's no such thing as a mental illness that is easy to recover from. They all suck. They are all some of the largest sticks in the ass you can imagine. Panic disorder is closest to my heart because I suffered with it for so long. Every chapter in this book provides good advice to help you recover from a mental illness, especially anxiety, but there are certain steps you must take that are specific to anxiety and panic disorder.

- **Understand that you can recover.** Please trust me when I tell you wholeheartedly that if I can recover, so can you. I know that sounds like such a cliché, but it's true. I suffered with some of the worst anxiety and panic that you can ever imagine. I could barely leave the house comfortably. I lost friends. I lost jobs. I lost my whole life. Recovery is definitely possible. Please trust me. You can get better. I'm pulling for you.
- **Get the right help.** You need to do what works best for you. For me, again, it was exposure therapy, or doing the things that brought on anxiety, which was pretty much everything. Driving farther away from home. Riding in elevators. Driving on the highway. Talking to people. Going into a busy restaurant. Going to the supermarket. Pretty much any experience—I either had anxiety about it or was afraid I would have a panic attack in that situation. Exposure therapy is entering these situations with a "safe" person and learning to work through the fear. After

that, it was going into these situations by myself and each time staying longer and longer until it didn't faze me. If another type of therapy works better for you, then go for it.
- **Don't be afraid of medication.** Anxiety and panic attacks bring on very real and extremely uncomfortable bodily sensations. Medication can reduce the symptoms and make life easier. It can even allow you to function again. Make sure to work with a psychiatrist who specializes in anxiety disorders. I'm not afraid to say I needed medication to recover. I still rely on it. Anxiety disorder is a real condition that is rooted in brain chemistry, genetics, and our environment. It is as real as heart disease or cancer. You would take medication for those ailments, so why wouldn't you take them for a mental illness?
- **Find support.** I can't speak highly enough about talking with other people who are going through this at the same time you are. It can be great to share your wins and struggles with individuals who truly understand. You'll also learn tips and tricks about what works and what doesn't for other people, which can definitely help you in your own recovery. Just be cautious not to get dragged down or deflated when other people want to give up or get too negative.
- **Find your "safe" person.** In the beginning, it's very important to have a person or multiple

people whom you feel safe around. These are people you trust, usually a spouse or best friend, who will help you enter the triggering situation. They will help push you but also be there to support and comfort you when the physical symptoms become too overwhelming.
- **Use your tools.** One of the things that helped me the most was my bag of tools that distracted me from how I was feeling. Picture this: everywhere I went I had this big blue backpack, and it was stuffed with more stuff than you can imagine. It had water bottles, candy, games, books, and a lot of other things. Whenever I began to feel the symptoms of anxiety, I would take out one of these items and use it as a distraction. Getting your mind off of how you are feeling is key. In time, you won't need all the tools. In the beginning, do whatever works.
- **Take small steps.** My battle with panic disorder involved a series of very small steps that got bigger and bigger. Sometimes when I'd take these small steps forward and start to feel pretty comfortable about something, I'd get knocked on my ass and lose some of the ground I had gained. Even when this happens, just keep pushing. Focus on putting one foot in front of the other, even metaphorically—baby steps.
- **Rejoice in the victories.** One of the greatest feelings in the world is when you step through

the fear and do something in spite of it. I do a lot of public speaking, but even to this day every time I get on a stage I feel anxiety. I even have moments when I'm thinking to myself, "I can't do this today." I do it anyway. It is the best freaking feeling in the world when you kick your anxiety in the ass. It builds the ultimate self-confidence and self-esteem. It makes you feel like you are on top of the world and can do anything. Guess what? You can!

- **Practice your keister off.** Recovering from an anxiety disorder is like anything else—the more practice and effort you give it, the better the results. It's not easy. It's going to knock you on your ass. You'll feel tired and beat up. Just keep practicing and moving forward. With all the hard work, don't forget to give yourself some downtime once in a while to recover.
- **F*ck it.** Yes, this is a real tip. One of my counselors and friends would always say this to me. I would be talking to her about a particular situation that was causing me distress, and she would just look at me and say, "F*ck the fear and do it anyway!"[9]

---

9   This chapter is not intended to be taken as medical advice. If you struggle with anxiety or panic disorder, work with your own medical doctor to create an individualized treatment plan.

Part 3

REFLECTIONS ON LIFE AND PARENTING AND SOME OTHER RANDOM THOUGHTS FROM BRUCE

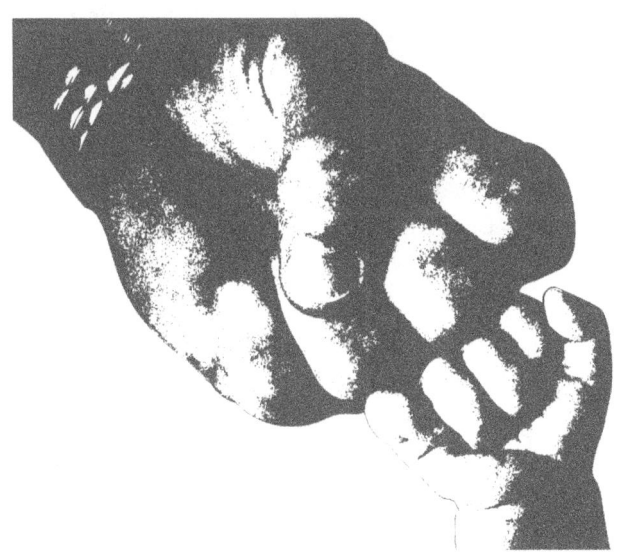

BIRTHDAYS ROCK!

> The way I see it, you should live every day like it's your birthday.
>
> —Paris Hilton

My daughter's best friend turned 13 years old recently. My daughter told me that her friend woke up at 5:00 A.M. and couldn't go back to sleep because she was so excited that it was her birthday. At first, I was kind of confused. Then it hit me: this makes a ton of sense.

When did birthdays become something we dread?

I remember just how fun birthdays were growing up. When I was a kid, we used to have our birthday parties at the roller-skating rink or McDonald's. It was something I looked forward to all year long. Everything about it was just awesome: the gifts, the party, my friends, the cake, and just a day full of fun celebrating me.

But then, something happened along the way. As the years went by, getting older wasn't fun anymore, and I stopped looking forward to those birthdays. In fact, like many others, I began to dread them. How many times have you told people you are turning 20 or 30 again? Not only are birthdays now a reminder of getting older, but as someone who doesn't usually like to be the center of attention, I just hated having to hear about it all day long, even though everyone obviously had good intentions. I also hated going out to eat and having someone get up and pretend to use the restroom, just to go tell the restaurant staff it was my birthday so they would come over, singing, with a dessert.

Live it up and reclaim your birthday fun.

A few years ago, I decided to approach it very differently. I pulled the stick out of my ass, and instead of treating my birthday as something to dread, I welcomed it and even embraced it. I'm not talking about the usual bullshit like "You don't get older; you get better" or "Wisdom comes with age." I'm talking about using my birthday as a day for me to do whatever I want and to really celebrate me. Sometimes that means doing nothing at all but lounging around, and other times that means taking a trip or doing something fun. And sometimes, it means just going about my usual business.

The point is, instead of dreading it and getting depressed about it, I welcome it with open arms. And the singing in the restaurant with the cake? Bring it on! It's my day, and it's time to celebrate.

PULL THE STICK OUT OF YOUR @$$

Forget about the number behind your birthday, even if you're entering a new decade. Don't get upset over it. Don't get down and depressed. Don't fight it. Don't think about the fat and calories that come from a delicious-tasting birthday cake. Welcome your birthday. Get excited. Think back to all the fun you had when you were a kid. Make it fun again. Celebrate you! Have a second and third piece of cake. You know what else? I hope you get presents. I think you should give presents to other people on their birthday. I think it's stupid when people say, "Don't bring presents." I always do anyway.

As I write this, I'm celebrating my 44th birthday. Hard to believe? Yes, a little bit. Upsetting? Heck no. I'm going to have fun and enjoy every minute of it. If today is your birthday, happy birthday! Go have the time of your life. Pull the stick out of your ass and live it up, celebrating you by doing whatever it is that makes you happy.

HO HO HO, OH NO, NOT THE HOLIDAY SEASON

> Go, and redeem some other promising young creature, but leave me to keep Christmas in my own way.
> —Ebenezer Scrooge

It's supposed to be "the most wonderful time of the year." Unfortunately, for many people, including myself, the holidays are tough. I know, I know… I need to pull the stick out of my ass and try to find some Christmas cheer.

I like Halloween. I also really enjoy Thanksgiving. By the time the Hanukkah and Christmas season comes around, however, I think I'm just done. Life is stressful and challenging enough, and the holidays just seem to complicate things even more, making me feel as if I'm falling behind. Shopping, decorating, traveling during this busy period, family get-togethers, office parties, and other social gatherings aren't my thing and take a toll on me. People who suffer with a mental illness can have an especially difficult time during the holidays, and I think many people who don't have a true diagnosed condition struggle as well. For me, the best way I find joy in the season is watching my kids find joy in it.

There goes Mr. Humbug.

I'm working on it. I'm trying to get better. It's a big stick that's way up there for me. I'm trying to complain less to my wife, who really gets into the holidays. I don't want to take away her joy. I'm far from perfect and probably never will be. And that's okay. Here are the stick-pulling steps I take to feel better and try to be the best I can during this time of year. Hopefully it helps you, too.

- **Don't beat yourself up over it.** Some people like things that other people don't. That's just life. Hey, after all, I like Barry Manilow. I always used to beat myself up over not being able to get into the spirit of the season. I pulled that stick out a long time ago, and I'm more accepting of it now.
- **Focus on what you do like.** I focus on the parts of the holidays that I do like, such as the food, nicely decorated homes, and other festive displays—and of course, watching my kids have fun.
- **Minimize the complaining.** I don't like complainers, but I become one every year my wife asks me to hang the Christmas lights. I've

realized she doesn't like to hear my whining, so I try to minimize it and keep it to myself.
- **Stay focused on work and life.** Many people seem to turn off completely come December, and I can't. Don't get me wrong: everyone needs a little time off, but concentrating on the usual day-to-day tasks helps me stay focused and connected to reality.
- **Reduce your stress.** It's a stressful time of the year. Stress is a killer and always need to be reduced—even more so during the holidays. Whatever you do to reduce stress, put an extra focus on it during the holiday months. Make time to relax, unwind, and recharge every single day.
- **Talk about it.** Like always, holding in how you're feeling during the holidays is never a good idea. It feels good to talk about any stress or frustration and get it off your chest. My great friend Andy is not much of a fan of the holidays, either, so I'll sit and vent about how I'm feeling to him, and it makes me feel so much better.
- **Don't overextend yourself.** There's so much going on during the holiday season and it's easy to overextend yourself. Commit only to what you are truly comfortable taking on. Remember, there are 24 hours in a day—no more, no less. It's okay to decline certain invitations or tell people "no." On a related note, don't neglect your sleep,

especially when you have a lot going on the next day.
- **Block it out temporarily.** Sometimes it just gets to be too much and I need a break from anything holiday related. One of my favorite things to do is to hop in my car, roll down the windows, and turn on some really upbeat rock music. I drive off the beaten path where there are no signs of Santa Claus, elves, or gingerbread men.
- **Stay on your meds.** I'm not embarrassed to talk about my need for psychiatric medication. Nobody should be. It's no different than taking heart or cold medication. The holiday season is not the best time to discontinue taking your meds. I don't rely on my anti-anxiety medication much anymore, but it is a lifesaver for me during the month of December and other very stressful times of the year.

"The holidays come but once a year," as a modified version of the old adage goes. While you might say "hell yes—thankfully" to this, you can still enjoy the holidays by resisting the pressure to put on a jolly façade and keeping them in your own way.

YOU'RE NEVER REALLY READY TO BE A PARENT

> At the end of the day, the most overwhelming key to a child's success is the positive involvement of a parent.
>
> —Jane Dee Hull

I remember when my wife got pregnant the first time. Talk about a wild roller coaster of emotions! It's both exciting and scary at the same time. You try to reassure yourself by thinking you have nine months to prepare, but who are you kidding? Those nine months fly by, and before you know it your life is turned upside down. Like seriously upside down.

The thing is, no matter how much you prepare—no matter how many books you read, or how many parenting classes you attend, or how much you talk to other people—you are never really ready. It's like you're just cruising along, thinking you are starting to figure out life, and then *BOOM!*—your whole world is rocked. It puts a stick up your derrière like you can't imagine, and I don't think this one ever comes out.

You learn as you go.

I remember the very first night home with my daughter, Taylor. It's midnight and she's crying. My wife and I were just looking at each other like "What the heck do we do?" So, we bailed. We went next door to the neighbor, who had two grown kids and loved babies. We're like, "Hey, it's midnight and all, but our baby is crying. Can you help?" She calmed her right down like it was nothing. Of course, six months later and a little crying, and we were pros. We still laugh about that. Can you believe we bothered this poor lady at midnight?

That's really the story of parenting right there. At first you are clueless. You learn as you go. You make a lot of mistakes. Then you make some more mistakes. You think you have one thing figured out, but then you're faced with a completely new scenario. It's a never-ending cycle that goes on forever. I think my parents still feel this way about me even though I'm a grown adult.

The point is, you're never really ready to be a parent. You kind of just figure it out as you go and learn from all your mistakes. Somehow, in the end, despite all your failures, doubts, and mixed emotions, you pull it off, and there's this little version of you that you've successfully managed to bring into this world.

It's not all rainbows and Hallmark specials.

Having kids is life-changing and like nothing you can imagine. They are truly the greatest. There's something so special that all parents feel but oftentimes can't put into words. Is it all fun and games and the biggest joy in life, like some people say? Heck no. Anyone who says that is delusional. People are often taken aback when I say this, but it's the truth. I love my kids. They mean the world to me, and I would do anything for them. I always try to be there for them. I try to help them. I do the best I can for them. But sure, there are times where you're going to be feeling anything but joy. You'll be tired, delirious, and wishing this kid would just go to sleep and stay asleep for a few hours. You'll have doubts, fears, uncertainties, and even question if you made the right choice to have kids. You'll have days you won't even know what the heck you're doing and feel like you are just winging it. And you will be. That's normal. You're not weird or different for having these feelings. Every parent has them, even if some will never admit it. So yes, parenting is one of the greatest joys in the world, but it can also make you incredibly uptight and stressed out.

By the way, for the people who say that once you have one kid it's not any more difficult to have more—are you kidding me? Who's the genius who came up with this one? It absolutely is a lot more work, and a lot more money, too. Also, whoever said that you will become a pro at changing those poopy diapers was lying. They never get any easier. Period. End of story.

Tips for enjoying the good parenting days and getting through the bad ones:

- **Enjoy it as much as you can.** The time goes by fast.
- We all get caught up in our work, in doing stuff around the house and other things, but **when your kids want your attention, give it to them as much as you can.** I'm far from perfect on this, and I'm not saying it's always possible. Kids need to feel wanted, and giving them attention accomplishes this and is just something you should be doing anyway.
- **There will be days where you don't want to deal with your kids. That doesn't mean you are a bad parent.** That's perfectly normal, so don't beat yourself up over your negative thoughts and feel guilty about having them. Parenting is a lot of work, and kids can be a royal pain in the heinie sometimes.

- **Kids don't care about money.** This is one I struggle with because I want to be able to give them "things." Sure, at times, these things (usually toys) bring them joy. But your kids really just want to be with you and have experiences. As Abigail Van Buren's famous (and accurate) line goes: "If you want your children to turn out well, spend twice as much time with them and half as much money."
- **Listen to your kids.** They're far from always right, but they just want to have a voice.
- **You're going to have to do things you don't want to do but that they will love**, and that's just life. Like camping. I hate camping more than anything. I went twice with my daughter. She claims to have liked it. I was miserable. I did it to spend time with her.
- **You're not always going to understand your kids.** That's okay. They have wild imaginations and want to invite you into their world. Go along with it.
- **You don't have to be perfect**, because you're already perfect in their eyes. And really, there's no such thing as perfect anyway.
- **Enjoy your time by yourself.** You'll desperately need it to relax, recharge, and keep your sanity.
- **Steer your kids, but don't make all their decisions for them.** My daughter has some friends that I think are really great and others with

whom I wish she wasn't friends. Obviously, if I really feel there is someone she shouldn't be hanging around with, I will say something. If it's harmless and I just don't like certain things about a friend of hers, I'm not going to stop her from being friends with the person. I simply steer her toward her other friends.

- **Protect your kids, but let them make their own mistakes.** Of course you want the very best for your children. Sometimes, though, the very best thing you can do is to back off. This is a tough one to come to terms with, but it's the truth.
- **Let your kids discover their own likes and talents.** My daughter loves lacrosse. My son likes art. I try to introduce them to other things, but I let them follow their passions. Never force your kids to do something they don't want to do.
- **Before you react, think back to when you were a kid.** When your child asks you to take her for ice cream, your knee-jerk reaction is probably to say "no" because you immediately think of the sugar, money, standing in line, and so on that's involved. But stop for a minute, and think back to when you were a child. Go for the ice cream.

SOME OTHER RANDOM BUT IMPORTANT STUFF

> Expose yourself to as much randomness as possible.
> —Ben Casnocha

It's my goal to keep this book short and to the point without becoming too overwhelming, but there are a few more important topics I quickly want to touch on that will also help you pull the stick out of your ass. They are in no particular order.

1. **Don't be influenced by the world around you.** Pay attention only to the world that you create for yourself. Getting lost in the gossip, what the media is talking about, and other people's reality is only taking you away from your real world, the one you create and want to live in.
2. **Don't be a control freak.** I had to have control over everything. I couldn't even be a passenger in a car it was so bad. I no longer have a control

stick up my ass. The key is to give up control little by little. Eventually, you'll come to realize that you don't need to exert control because you really already have control in most things you do.

3. **Don't judge a book by its cover.** This should be common sense by now, but sadly, so many people still screw this one up. It's easy to make presumptions just on appearance alone, but resist the urge—because what you see is not always what you get.

4. **Don't let people shit on you.** I wrote a whole chapter in this book about not shitting on yourself. At the same time, don't let people shit on you. I've taken crap more times than I care to recall, and I've had to be deliberate about protecting myself more. I'm still not always successful on this front, but I'm getting better. Always be nice and give people the benefit of the doubt, but when it becomes obvious that you're constantly being treated poorly, it's time to be a better advocate for yourself and cut any toxic ties.

5. **Don't talk down to people.** Words are powerful. What comes out of your mouth can literally make or break someone. It can propel them to greatness or crush them, leaving them lost, unsure of themselves, and paralyzed. Sometimes we say things we wish we didn't say. We've all done it. In general, though, do your best not

to talk down to people. And if you catch yourself doing it, apologize quickly and genuinely.
6. **There are three rules to a clean house.** These guidelines will save you time and your sanity, regardless of what my wife or anyone else says:
    - All dishes, no matter what they are made out of, go in the dishwasher.
    - All clothes, regardless of color or material, go in the washer and dryer.
    - The vacuum sucks up everything on the floor.

    I'm kidding, but really...

7. **Keep things simple.** Making life unnecessarily complex is one of the reasons why so many of us are walking around anxious and stressed out all the time. We're a society that's proud of our ability to multitask and cram as much shit as possible into a 24-hour period. Instead, take things slow, keep it simple, and enjoy the ride.
8. **The Joneses are dead, so stop trying to keep up with them.** Stop caring so much what other people think. Stop living your life for your friends, neighbors, or anyone else. Do the things you want to do. Wear the clothes you want to wear. Drive the car you want to drive. Decorate your home the way you want it to look. Think for yourself. Follow what you believe is right. Be original. Whatever you're doing, do it for you and you alone.

9. **There's no such thing as normal.** Schools have guidelines that determine what is "normal" or on grade level, above average, and below grade level. Our careers are ranked by titles and money earned. Parents of babies and toddlers are always comparing their kids to other kids. "My son can already say 10 words." "My girl was potty trained before she descended from my uterus." Throughout our lives, we're constantly matched up against other people in all that we do. Just pull the stick out of your ass and focus on you and your life, because the truth is, there's no such thing as normal.
10. **Treat everyone the same.** Why do we discriminate? Why do we show such hatred toward other people who are different than us? What's the big deal about holding different beliefs around religion, politics, sexual attraction, or anything else? It's amazing that in this day and age, this is such an issue in society. Don't for a second tell me that's just the way you were raised. Don't tell me that's what your religion instructs you to do. Don't make any lame excuses. If you can't treat everyone with love and kindness, then you have way more than just a stick up your ass. You're an asshole.
11. **Introverts are special people.** It always makes me laugh when I hear people talk about how being introverted is a bad thing. I used to think

that, too, but I was wrong. Introverts rule. Don't confuse introversion with social anxiety. They are very different. Introverts are not social phobic; they just need their quiet time to themselves. Introverts are usually super observant, great listeners, trustworthy, and can get things done on their own.

12. **You will never make everyone happy.** It's impossible. You can be the type of person who will do anything to appease others, agree with them even when deep down you disagree, say you like the things they like when you really don't, and just totally suck up to them all the time. Guess what? You still won't make them happy. Even more, you can be the type of person who doesn't like to rock the boat, never makes a controversial statement, and just tries to conform to the rules of society, and people will still find things they don't like about you. That's why it's best to pull the stick out of your ass and do the things that make you happy.

13. **There's no right way to grieve.** Grief is one of the most painful feelings anyone can experience. What makes it worse is other people telling you how you need to grieve. Even if they are well-intentioned, ignore them. Maybe you want to be alone. Maybe you want to be with others. Maybe you just want to go about your business as usual. Just know that whatever you do, there's no right

or wrong way to grieve. Also, remember there is no timeline on grief. How long does grief last? The answer to that is it never stops.

14. **Always give yourself something to look forward to.** It doesn't matter if it's a vacation, a night out, going skiing for the day, or anything else. When you can look forward to something about which you are genuinely excited, it helps keep those sticks away and puts you in a better frame of mind—happier and more optimistic.

15. **Life can be f*cking hard.** You know what I can't stand? People who want you to believe that life is easy. Life is never easy, even when you catch some good breaks. The sooner you realize that life is challenging for everyone—and I mean everyone—the more prepared you'll be to take it on. Don't get me wrong: life is great, but it's definitely not easy. With that said, give yourself a pat on the back every once in a while for doing as well as you have.

Conclusion

DON'T SIT ON IT: PULL THAT STICK OUT OF YOUR ASS IMMEDIATELY!

> Only I can change my life. No one can do it for me.
> —Carol Burnett

I hope you enjoyed reading this book as much as I liked writing it. I hope you learned a few things from my stories and life lessons. I hope you got a laugh or two. Most importantly, I hope you were able to identify parts of your life where you have a proverbial stick up your ass and you're now taking the steps to pull it out and lighten up.

One thing I've noticed is that it's usually pretty easy to tell where in your life you are struggling. You probably know exactly where you need to pull the stick out, but what you might be having difficulty with is *how* to go about doing it. That's why I wrote this section—to help you get started.

Everyone's situation is different. What one person is currently dealing with might be very different from what someone else is going through. Nonetheless, whatever issues you are facing right now, there are some steps you can take to lighten the load, feel better, and enjoy your life more. These are my 10 commandments to living a freer, more relaxed life.

1. **Get real with yourself.** You know what your problem areas are, and now it's up to you to do something about them. Whatever it is that's got you down, is standing in the way of your success and happiness, and is therefore a major stick in the ass, figure out how you're going to deal with it. Ignoring it won't make it get any better.
2. **Lighten up.** This is something that can help all of us, especially if you tend to be uptight, worry about everything, take things too seriously, analyze things in great detail, are stressed out all the time, complain about every little detail, and just can't relax. Make it a goal to lighten up as much as you can.
3. **Have more fun.** Whatever your definition of fun is, do more of it. That's what life is really all about.
4. **Relax more.** Life is stressful. You probably have a lot on your plate. Whatever you are going through, you need to find ways to reduce your

stress and relax more. It's important for both your mental and physical health. There are many great ways to do this. Do whatever works best for you.
5. **Live life on your own terms.** Forget how your friends, family, or anyone else wants you to live your life. Don't be influenced by the way society wants you to think. Ignore the talking heads on TV. Pay less attention to the garbage on social media. Live your life how you want to live it. Do what you love. Follow your passions.
6. **Recognize when you need help.** There are many strategies and coping techniques you can do on your own that will help you feel better. Sometimes, however, you can't do it on your own. Recognize when it's time to get help from a qualified mental health professional like a psychologist, psychiatrist, social worker, or counselor. Therapy, medication, and alternative treatments can make a world of difference.
7. **Do whatever works.** When it comes to feeling better, there is no right or wrong answer and there is no one-size-fits-all solution. Whatever works best for you is what you should continue to pursue.
8. **Love yourself.** Be proud of who you are and what you stand for, even when other people disagree. Be your own best friend, and learn to comfort yourself.

9. **Have more good days than bad ones.** Everyone has bad days. To think you can avoid them is unrealistic. Do your best to have more good days than bad ones. When the bad ones come around, just do what you have to do to get through them. When the good ones come around, enjoy the heck out of them.
10. **Stop putting life on hold.** I don't know what's coming five years from now, next year, or next month. Heck, I don't even know what tomorrow will bring. Today is all you've got. Get out there, and start doing the things you want to do now. Don't wait for retirement. Don't wait for the kids to get older. Do it now!

This is by no means a fully comprehensive list of things you can do, but it gives you some simple steps you can take to begin pulling the stick out of your ass and to start feeling better and improving your life. There are many other great strategies out there, and I'm sure you have some of your own that work best for you. Whether it's anxiety, depression, stress—something mental health-related or otherwise—these are some pretty solid suggestions that will make your life a lot better and more fulfilling and will help you no matter what you are going through.

Again, I wish you the absolute best in your journey, and a life full of happiness, laughter, and great things to come.

Mental Health Resources

PULL THE STICK OUT OF YOUR @$$

NATIONAL SUICIDE PREVENTION LIFELINE

Call 1-800-273-8255
or chat with a counselor online.

Free support available 24 hours a day.

CRISIS TEXT LINE

Text HOME to 741741
to text with a trained crisis counselor.

Free support available 24 hours a day.

232

ANXIETY AND DEPRESSION ASSOCIATION OF AMERICA

Visit https://adaa.org/living-with-anxiety/ask-and-learn/resources.

NATIONAL ALLIANCE ON MENTAL ILLNESS

Visit nami.org.
Call the NAMI helpline at 1-800-950-6264, or if in a crisis **text** NAMI to 741741.

PULL THE STICK OUT OF YOUR @$$

THE NATIONAL INSTITUTE OF MENTAL HEALTH INFORMATION RESOURCE CENTER

Visit nimh.nih.gov.
Call 1-866-615-6464,
or talk to a representative online.

234

THE ANXIETY AND PHOBIA PROGRAM AT ST. VINCENT'S BEHAVIORAL HEALTH CENTER

Visit http://www.phobia-anxiety.org/.
Call 914-286-4430.

ACKNOWLEDGMENTS

To Susanna, Taylor, & Grayson: The greatest thing in life is having you all by my side every day. Never stop laughing, chasing your dreams, and being who you are. I love you forever.

To Mom & Dad: Thank you for always being there for me and for all your love and guidance over the years. I love you.

To Seth Kaplan: Thank you for your friendship all of these years. Thank you for being my grammar god and sharing the TV news bug with me. I think the police in Nassau still have nothing to go on.

To Andy Fleece: Everyone should be as lucky as I am to have a friend like you. Thanks for always being there for me and believing in me even when I don't believe in myself.

To Judy Shaw: Look how far I've come. It would not have been possible without you.

To Steve Siebold: Thank you for your friendship all of these years and teaching me about mental toughness. You'll always be the guy who won five majors on the PGA Tour in one year.

To Eric Rittmeyer: You are the definition of perseverance and kindness. Thank you for your friendship.

To Dr. Alok Trivedi: Thanks for being a friend and mentor all these years. I love watching you take an idea and turn it into something big.

To Chris Lavoro: The master ping pong ball spinner, halfway decent golfer, and best espresso maker out there. Thanks for your friendship.

To Brian Roberts: Thanks for helping me keep my sanity in this crazy world. I'm so glad we're friends.

To Rob & Kerri Stuart: Thank you for being the best travel agents and video production crew out there. Most importantly, thank you for your friendship.

To Sandra Larson: Thanks for being a great friend all these years and the world's best graphic designer and IT support.

To Everyone at Sound Wisdom: Thank you for believing in me and my vision for this book. Thank you for all of your hard work in making it happen. I couldn't have done it without you.

www.ingramcontent.com/pod-product-compliance
Lightning Source LLC
Chambersburg PA
CBHW070142100426
42743CB00013B/2793